JOURNEY to the BAY

Jim Doherty & Joe O'Donnell

BRANDON

First published in 1991 by
Brandon Book Publishers Ltd
Cooleen, Dingle, Co. Kerry.

© James Doherty & Joseph O'Donnell

British Library Cataloguing in Publication Data
Doherty, J.E. (James E)
  Journey to the Bay.
  I. Title II. O'Donnell, Joseph
  823.914 [J]

ISBN 0-86322-136-X

This book is published with the financial assistance of the Arts Council/An Chómhairle Ealaíon, Ireland

Cover illustration: Ray Mullan
Cover design: John Brady
Typeset by Brandon
Printed and bound in Great Britain by
The Guernsey Press Co. Ltd, Guernsey, Channel Islands.

MAP

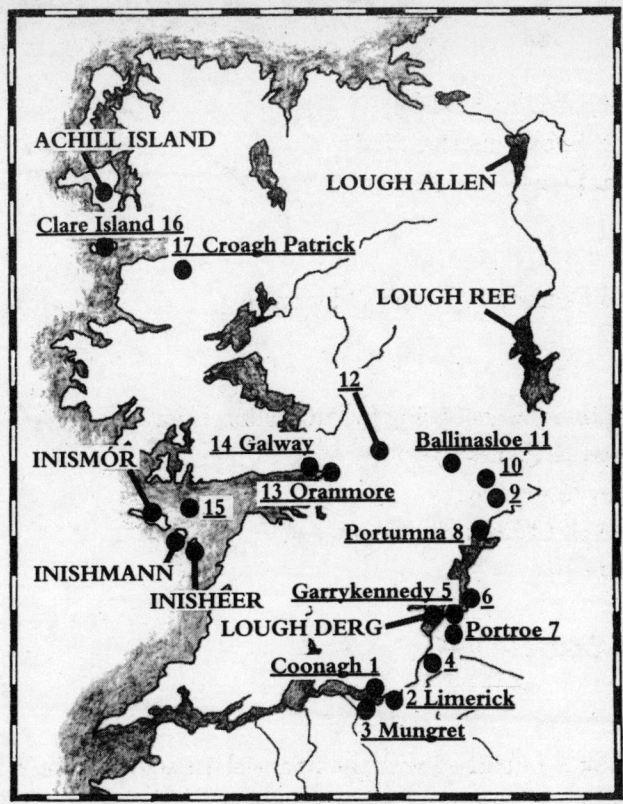

KEY TO THE MAP

1. Coonagh, Turlough's birthplace
2. Limerick city, surrendered to Ireton on 27 October 1651
3. Mungret, where Turlough is captured by slavers
4. Cragg and Gooig, the home of Eamon O'Riain, who rescues Turlough from the slavers
5. Garrykennedy, where Turlough rests with McNamara
6. Dromineer, where a large crowd attends Mass at the Rock
7. Portroe, burned by Roundheads
8. Portumna, where Turlough is helped by O'Halloran
9. The wood where Turlough is attacked by wolves and recaptured by the slavers
10. Where Turlough makes his bid to escape
11. Ballinasloe Fair
12. Where Turlough is reunited with O'Riain
13. Outside Oranmore Turlough meets Rhattican the bard
14. Galway and the Claddagh
15. The battle of the ships
16. Clare Island and the Bay of Islands
17. Croagh Patrick, the holy mountain

I

WHEN TURLOUGH heard the thunder of the horses' hooves he looked around. Bran Óg barked at him from a hillock, then put his head to one side as if to hear better. Turlough's temples pounded as his eyes searched for the horsemen. The earth shook. He began to run towards the cabin, glancing wildly to all sides, feeling that at any moment the horses would be upon him. Then, with a shriek that could be heard into the peak of the sky, the horses broke cover. Hundreds upon hundreds of them raced across the hillside. They were so far away it seemed that they were standing still, poised in gallop. Now, in a fan-like movement they rode madly across the hill, small horses with small riders, galloping in the direction of Limerick.

Turlough awoke drenched in sweat. The cabin was silent: he could not even hear the breathing of his parents at the other end of the room. He threw off the old cloak and sat up but he could see nothing, nor was there any noise, even from outside. Then he heard a faint stirring. There was the sound of his father clearing his throat.

"Turlough," his mother said quietly.

"Mam."

"Go back to sleep like a good boy."

He pulled the cloak around him and lay back. It seemed an age before he lost consciousness.

In the morning his father had gone. Turlough found his mother standing outside the door looking across the river. The Shannon was in flood. This was the time she hated.

For a moment she did not notice him. Then she started out of her vigil and whirled around. Her smile lit up her pale face and hid the dark circles around her eyes. She pulled back the head-dress of her cloak, freeing her hair to fall across her shoulders.

He had always heard people say that his mother was tall for a woman. When he was younger she boasted that the O'Malley women were as tall and strong as men and she told stories of the great Granuaile, Grace O'Malley, whom no man would defy except at his peril. Now, although he was little more than twelve years old, Turlough was as tall as she. He resembled his mother in looks. They had the same sharp cast of features, with green observant eyes. Their hair was the same dark red, although his mother's was long while his was tightly-cropped and curling. In one way their faces were very different. Turlough's was freckled from his life in the open but his mother's, once dark in complexion, was now pale and worried. It was always said to him that he took his shape from his father's people. He had the long legs of the O'Briens and their confident walk. His broad shoulders and deep chest promised a great adult strength.

"Is he gone?" Turlough asked.

"He'll not be long," she said, but she sounded weary.

"Where is the fighting now?"

His mother shook her head. "God help us, who can tell?" She turned and went back to the cabin.

He stood alone and looked towards the Shannon. It seemed no length of time since he had stood here with his father, listening to the guns from Penn's ships at Bunratty. The nights after that had been filled with hushed stories of the slaughter committed by Penn's troops. During the day the smoke curled in the air and at night they watched the fires of burning cabins licking the sky. He remembered the despair etched on his neighbours' faces when they heard of the battle of Six Mile Bridge where the Confederate army was cut to pieces by the army of the Parliament. He shivered. The war was very close now.

He returned to the cabin. Milk and oatcake and cheese were laid out for him.

"God save you!"

Turlough looked up. He knew well the gruff sound of their nearest neighbour, McMahon.

"Is himself around?" McMahon asked.

"He's out on the river this while," his mother replied. She looked at the fat man expectantly.

"Is he on his own?"

"Seán's with him."

"Better to have three than two these times," McMahon said sourly. He stood in the middle of the floor, watching the two of them from under his lowered eyebrows.

"Is there trouble?" she asked.

"No more than usual." McMahon was terse, but Turlough could tell that there was more on his mind. "I hear the eldest lad of the McMahons over the way was killed last night," he said after a while.

"Lord have mercy on him."

"He's a cousin of my own and I wondered if himself might have heard anything."

Turlough's mother shook her head. "And what happened?"

"Found dead in a ditch, they say. Some trooper maybe looking for a bit of sport found him and ..." McMahon made a harsh clicking sound with his tongue.

"Poor lad." She made the Sign of the Cross and looked anxiously across the room at her son.

Turlough realised that the chances of going off for the day with his dog, Bran Óg, had vanished. He sighed. He was determined to escape for a few hours.

He watched as his mother waited for McMahon to say more but the fat man just stood in front of them without making any sound. Then, turning suddenly, he nodded to them and, muttering to himself, he left the cabin. They listened until the heavy sound of his footsteps faded away.

Turlough's mother sat by the fire. He knew her thoughts were on McMahon's news. She brooded on the troubles around them. She would start thinking of her own people in Mayo and the life she had enjoyed there so many years ago, before she came to Limerick. And in this mood she would have nothing to say nor would she notice if he disappeared for a while. He signalled to Bran Óg and they slipped out to the hillside.

He spent the afternoon there with his friend Tomás McInerney. They raced around the hills, Turlough playing as Hugh Dubh O'Neill and Tomás as the enemy, Cromwell. When they tired of that they told each other stories they had overheard about the soldiers, as Bran Óg and Tomás's dog chased each other round their feet. Eventually, Turlough's stomach told him it was time to go home. If he was lucky his mother would not have noticed his absence, and if his father and Uncle Seán were back from the river her mind would be too occupied to question him. They were not home when he reached the cabin, but before his mother had time to start giving out to him they arrived.

Uncle Seán burst in first, laughing and holding up some of the day's catch. Turlough's mother took the fish silently and set about preparing the meal. Uncle Seán was older than Turlough's father. His hair, little as there was of it, was grey and his brown weather-beaten face was wrinkled. He was small and slim. Turlough's father was bigger and broader, and had a fine crop of brown hair. They made a contrasting pair as they sat talking.

While they sat down to a meal of fish and potatoes Turlough listened to the men's banter. When they had finished eating they moved over towards the fire and stretched out their feet. Silent now, they filled up their clay pipes and lit them. When the pipes were alight and the cabin filling up with the pungent aroma of tobacco, Turlough's father took a brown jug from the corner and poured a drink for himself and his brother.

Uncle Seán took the mug and solemnly examined it for a moment.

"They tell me there's strange things happening around Castleconnell." He paused, waiting until he had their attention. "A pedlar told me that you can hear noise and the sound of drinking and shouting at night. And there's music in the dark when there's nobody in the castle. They say the voices that are heard seem to be coming from Heaven as if the angels themselves were singing. And other times, the pedlar told me, you'll hear screeching like banshees; and people out that way say they hear men on foot and men on horseback when there's none there at all. The pedlar says there's no one able to get a wink of sleep around Castleconnell these times."

Turlough listened. His uncle's loud voice and good humour filled the room along with the aroma from the pipes which he and his brother were soberly smoking.

"And how is the great hunter?" Uncle Seán shouted, clapping Turlough on the knee.

Even Turlough's mother gave a smile. They all knew the story of the time Turlough and his uncle had gone into the woods to lure foxes. Seán had been teaching Turlough to stay absolutely still, moving the torch in a short slow arc until the foxes' curiosity gave them enough courage to approach. Then, when the fox was mesmerised by the light, the other hunter would reach out and catch the animal.

Uncle Seán had been using the torch; it had been Turlough's turn to grasp the animal by the back of the neck and then bind its feet. He had reached but the fox, snarling furiously, had taken him so much by surprise that he had lost his grip and the animal had disappeared in a flurry of yelps. Turlough had fallen over on his back, his feet in the air. Uncle Seán had laughed so much that he had lost his grip on the torch.

Angry with himself and blushing with shame, Turlough had tried to leave the wood on his own, but in the dark he had become confused. He had gone on only to become more and more lost, until Uncle Seán had finally located him. That had been his first time out luring foxes. There had been many other successful nights since, but that was the event everyone seemed to remember.

By now Turlough had learned to laugh at the adventure, but at the same time he wished that his parents and Uncle Seán would forget it.

"The mighty hunter is fine," he said.

"Ready for the wolf so," Seán said, winking at his brother.

Turlough's father expelled smoke from his mouth and smiled. "Time will tell," he said. "But in the meantime the mighty hunter has to be a mighty sailor tomorrow, so let him take to his bed."

"And there's the truth," Uncle Seán said. "I'd best be off to my wife and children for fear they take it into their heads I've been killed."

"God forbid!" said Turlough's mother as Uncle Seán left the cabin, shouting good night over his shoulder.

"And now, let the sailor take to his bed," his father repeated.

Turlough made his sleepy good nights and wrapped himself up for the night.

It seemed only minutes before his father was shaking him awake. They ate their oatmeal quickly and then quietly left the cabin for the river. Turlough enjoyed the river at this time, especially when it was like this, just the two of them. The horizon was streaked with the vivid colours of the dawn, a prelude to a warm day. But they had little time to admire the colours of the sky: there was hard work to be done.

They set to it. Turlough helped his father let out the net, rowing the boat in a long slow crescent on the water. Then, when they had completed the circuit, his father began to haul. Muscles stood out like cords on his long brown arms. Turlough compared the two sets of arms; his were brown but they lacked the leathery appearance of his father's. He stayed close to his father's side, watching as the glistening fish struggled in the coils of the net. When the catch was alongside the boat Turlough leaned down and began to lift out the fish. They glinted and twisted and writhed in his hands as he separated them and flung them into the bow. When the fish had all been landed, there was time for a short rest before they set about their labours again.

"What's the reason for all this fighting?" Turlough asked his father suddenly. He had asked him the same question before, too, but he never seemed to make sense of the answer.

His father's face was lined with thought. "We want to practise our religion," he said slowly, his voice hard. "That's what the Confederation of Kilkenny is fighting for."

Turlough thought of their priest, the gentle Fr O'Dwyer who had left Coonagh two years before. He had fled for his life. Turlough had good memories of him and of the occasional hours he had snatched from his duties to teach Turlough some Latin.

"Who is stopping us?" he asked after a while.

"The King of England cannot be trusted," his father said. "We gave him money so that we could be left alone with our religion, but he broke his word to us. Then he made promises to his own people in England but he didn't keep them either. He fights now with his own Parliament, and seeks help from our Confederation against his Parliament and against the Irish Parliament also. But who can trust such a man?" he spat out contemptuously. "And then there's the land. Our enemies want what land we have left. So there you have it. Land and religion. Religion and land."

"Then who is the Pope's man?" Turlough asked, remembering what his father and Uncle Seán had argued about one night.

"Rinuccini. He was sent to us from Rome by the Pope."

"How can he help us win?"

His father looked into the water. "I don't know the answer to that," he said.

"Can we win?" said Turlough, echoing a question he had heard his uncle ask.

"Only if we stay united. But we are not united. Eoin Roe O'Neill fights for the Confederation in Ulster and Thomas Preston fights for us in Leinster, but they would fight each other quicker than they would fight the Parliament. I've heard tell that those two hate each other so much that when they are in the one room men have to stand between them in case they kill each other."

"What's happening in Limerick now?"

His father scowled. "What indeed? That's a good tale, too. The Mayor and his Aldermen would make peace with the King. They would even give the city over to his man Ormond. But the Confederation will not have it."

"Why?"

"Because there is no trust in that King." His father looked at the empty net and smiled at the sight of the catch in the bottom of the boat. "We'll say no more about the war. Like your mother says, we still have to live, war or no war.

"A good day's work, thanks be to God." He clapped Turlough on the shoulder. "Whatever about foxes, you're a powerful fisherman for your age."

Turlough felt the warmth that always glowed when his father praised him. They turned for home.

Turlough was breathless with excitement as he ran up to the cabin to show his mother their day's work. He burst in through the door and stopped, panting. His father came in quietly behind him and pushed him gently to one side.

His mother's lips trembled and her eyes were red with crying. Turlough's father stood in front of her, waiting for her to speak.

"Seán!" she cried out.

"Seán?" his father repeated, looking at her.

"He's killed," she said.

His father moved back as though he had been hit. His face turned white. His throat worked as though he was choking. "Killed!"

"Killed," she repeated. "He's been killed. They found him dead this morning. They say he was killed with a knife in the belly."

His father grinned stupidly, looking from one of them to the other, searching for words.

"Soldiers?"

She nodded. "There's not much hope left for any of us if we stay in this place."

"We'll not leave everything we have here," Turlough's father said grimly.

"People are leaving for Limerick," his mother said.

"Let them."

"We should go!" his mother cried out.

"No." His jaw was tightly clenched.

"We should go," Turlough said with a sudden anger. "Mother is right. I hate it here!"

He felt his father's hand across his shoulder. For a moment it rested there. He could feel the tension in his father's body. His hand ruffled Turlough's hair for a moment before it fell back to hang limply by his side.

Turlough went outside the cabin and looked across the horizon where Uncle Seán's cabin was hidden behind the hills. He shivered at the thought of Uncle Seán laughing and telling his stories one night and then the next day lying cold in a field with a knife through his body. He shivered again as he thought of how warm he had felt when he stood beside his uncle with the torch blazing as they waited for the fox to make its timid advance. And in the boat sometimes when it was cold he had rested between his father and Uncle Seán, heated by the warmth of their bodies. He blinked and tears rolled down his cheeks.

His mother called out and pointed. They followed her gaze. Across the fields a blaze lit up the sky.

II

THEY BURIED Uncle Seán in the cold graveyard at the top of the headland where all the O'Briens of Coonagh were buried. From there they could see across to Cratloe with its woods; looking the other way they could follow the course of the river Shannon until it disappeared into mist. Somewhere in the distance, Turlough knew, was Limerick with its many walls and gates.

On their way home from the funeral they were silent, walking slowly in the cold morning air. Turlough felt a sense of relief as they neared their own place; here it would be warm. But as they approached the door of the cabin his mother gave a groan.

"I want to go home," she said.

"You are home," his father answered, catching her arm. He guided her towards the fire.

"No," she cried, "this is not my home. I hate this place. I want to go back home to Mayo."

"Hush," his father said. "Hush. Things will get better." But his father did not sound as if he believed what he was saying.

They sat by the fire for the evening.

"Do you remember when you came to Mayo first?" Turlough's mother asked quietly.

His father nodded. "I remember. I never thought there could be so many islands in one bay."

"It's so beautiful there," she said.

"It's beautiful here, is it not?"

"It's not the same. When you came first you even said that yourself. Have you forgotten?"

"No," he murmured. "I've not forgotten."

Turlough listened. It was one of his favourite stories. His father and Uncle Seán had decided to imitate their Danish ancestors and have a summer of adventure while they were still young enough to enjoy it, as they said.

They had left Coonagh to sail out along the Clare coast. But they had kept on going north, until they sailed into Galway Bay. The fishermen there had treated them with great suspicion and had made them unwelcome. The brothers had debated whether to return to Coonagh then, but had decided that they would continue to travel north. They had fished their way along the coast into Mayo and finally entered the Bay of Islands of the O'Malleys. With such a sea journey behind them they would have remembered that summer for the rest of their lives if nothing else had happened. But, to crown the adventure, Turlough's father had fallen in love with the tall red-haired girl whose family governed the Bay. He had wanted to bring her back for marriage in Coonagh, but her father would not hear of it: they would marry in Mayo or not at all, he had declared. And that was the way it was. At the end of the summer the two young men had returned, one of them married to the beautiful girl of the O'Malleys. Their story was told around firesides for years afterwards. Turlough had been listening to the tale for as long as he could remember.

He listened now to their tired voices. That summer seemed so far away.

"Is this a place to bring up a child?" his mother was chiding. "Who might be the next to die such ... such a death. Will it be you? Or Turlough, maybe?" She looked at her husband. He held his head down, and made no answer.

"We'll have to go from this place!"

"We can think on it for the night," Turlough's father answered slowly, "and talk again tomorrow."

"No!" she cried out. "If we stay in this place much longer there will be no tomorrow for us! It'll be Turlough or yourself buried up on the hill beside poor Seán. The wolf is loose across the land. Only last night we saw the sky lit up with fire from the cabin the soldiers burned. How far away was that, tell me?"

His father made no reply.

"If you don't leave this place, I'll go myself," she said after a while.

"And where will you go?" he asked impatiently. "Are they not everywhere, from Limerick out to Bunratty and beyond? If it isn't one crowd of them it's another. You've no business to go north. No one will get past Bunratty. One time it's the Parliament and then it's the Confederation, and now it's Ironsides from England. Do you think it makes any difference which way you go? And you think you'll make it to the Plains of Mayo!" he said scornfully.

"I don't care!" His mother's voice rose to an angry, desperate tone. "I'll go anywhere to get away from this hell of a place, with its fires and deaths and tortures, and children dying in the fields."

Turlough stared into the fire, holding his breath. Since childhood he had listened to his father proclaiming that this piece of Coonagh was his, the home of his Danish ancestors. He was proud of that - that he was an O'Brien with Danish blood in him. And he was proud, too, that it was the founder of the O'Briens, Brian Boru, who had defeated the Vikings at the Battle of Clontarf; and here, to this day, was a family with Danish and O'Brien blood fishing the Shannon and farming the land of Clare. "This is the land we have lived on since the time of Brian Boru," he would say with pride. But now, Turlough wondered, what would they do, now that the land around them had become dangerous for their very lives. Where once it had been peaceful, death was now their daily companion.

He was nodding into the fire. He made no movement when he felt himself being urged to his feet; he felt exhausted. His mother coaxed him to his bed, and he lay down. He could hear his father talking quietly in the darkness. And then, still waiting for some sign of his father's intention, he fell asleep.

By the time Turlough woke in the morning his father had left the cabin. His mother, standing by the smoking fire, watched him as he sat alone at the table, eating his oatmeal.

"I never thought 'twould come to this," she said eventually, speaking almost as if to herself. "We should have stayed with my people in Mayo. We were safe in the Bay of Islands. No one throws children off the land there. And there's enough fishing for Irish and English and all."

"Don't worry, Mother – he'll come to our way. It's just that he loves this place."

Her voice softened. "From Croagh Patrick itself, the Holy Mountain, you look across the wide sea and you face into the finest fishing grounds in the whole world. I heard my father say that and he should know. Did know," she corrected herself. "The land of Grace O'Malley, your own cousin. Do you remember I told you that?"

He nodded.

"Granuaile that not even the Queen of England on her throne could get the better of! We could have stayed there where we met, among my people. They would have seen him as one of their own. There are none to attack the O'Malleys of the Bay." She smiled to herself briefly. "Ah," she said, "nothing would do your father but we must settle in this place by the Shannon. And now look at the misfortune that's on us."

He sat in silence. He knew there was little point in interrupting her. She seemed to think for a long time before she spoke again, and when she did her voice was tired.

"Turlough, *a leana*, promise me something. Will you promise me something?" she asked wearily. She put her hand on his head, ruffling his hair, and he nodded. "If anything happens –

to your father and myself – you'll go to the O'Malleys in the Bay of Islands? To Mayo; to my people. You'll be safe there and they'll see to you. There'll be a life there for you, away from this murder and fire and fear."

"Nothing will happen to us," Turlough answered boldly. "Father will see to us through these times." He stared into her eyes and then looked away from her expression of dismay. "He says there'll be peace soon!"

"Does he?" she asked, as she moved back towards the fire. "This war won't end tomorrow or the day after. And that's not what I asked you. I asked you will you make your way to my people if any harm comes here."

"Don't worry, Mother," Turlough said. "We'll survive." He did not completely believe what he was saying.

"What will you do?" she asked sharply. "What will you fight with?"

Turlough looked around but all he could see were fishing poles.

"I'll get something."

"I'm sure you would, *a leana*. But you will need more than yourself. And what will you do? Will you live with the McMahons, maybe?"

"No."

"That's easy said. But there's no one else. Poor Seán is dead and his family must shift for themselves. There's no more of your father's people within easy reach of this place, and who knows what way they are by this time. Mayo will be the only safe place for you. You must promise me that you will make that journey – long as it is – from here to the Bay."

He thought of the stories she had told him of her home by the waters of the Atlantic in Clew Bay, and how her eyes had shone with delight as she talked. Many times she had described the Holy Reek where St Patrick had spent forty days and nights fast-ing. He had listened enthralled as she described the view from the mountain – of the land and seas and islands. The islands lived in his imagination: there was one for every day of the year, she had said.

"Isn't it a strange thing to think that I never seem to remember anything but war since I left Mayo to come here," his mother interrupted his thoughts. "Will you answer me now?"

"I will find someone to fight beside," Turlough said.

His mother shook her head. "Go to Mayo. You will find men to fight beside there: my brothers and their children and all your cousins. They will fight on land or sea. Will you promise me?" she pleaded.

Resolutely he said, "I promise, Mother. I will go."

She nodded with satisfaction and said no more.

When Turlough's father returned he looked anxiously at his wife. She placed his dinner on the table and waited for him to speak.

"The McMahons are going," he said as he bent over the plate of potatoes.

"Going where?"

"Limerick. He says they'll be safer there inside the walls than out here with the soldiers roaming loose."

"And what do you say?" his mother asked.

His father shrugged. "Maybe he's right, maybe he's not."

"He'll be where there's protection," she said impatiently.

"Protection!" His father slapped his hand on the table. "What protection? If Cromwell and the Ironsides come with their cannon what good will the walls of Limerick be then? The walls of the towns kept out the enemy when there was no cannon in the old days. But the walls of the towns are old and sick these times, and it won't take much to push them over."

"I don't care!"

"I'll go and see if they need any help with their journey," he stood up from the table. "You come with me, Turlough."

The McMahons' place was a short walk away. They had no children and Turlough seldom went there. He did not like the short, fat McMahon with his gruff voice who spoke only when he had to. He disliked the way McMahon seemed to rush at the world as if he was trying by force to fashion it to his will in the same way as he forced a cow, a horse or a dog into submission. McMahon's wife was small like her husband, but thin. She was friendly in a frightened sort of a way. She seemed afraid that at any moment someone was going to strike her.

McMahon saw them coming. He was heaving a sack of oats onto the cart while the donkey stood patiently waiting for the burden to be loaded.

"God save you," Turlough's father called out. McMahon grunted in response and continued with his labour.

"Where will you be staying?" Turlough's father asked.

"I've a cousin within in the town. He'll give us a corner for ourselves." He wiped the sweat from his face with his arm and looked at Turlough. "Maybe you'd want us to take the boy with us? He'd be safer there than out here."

Turlough stared at him in disbelief.

"There's only a few miles in it if anything happens," his father said, laughing.

"There wasn't more than a few miles in it for your brother to be whipped away or for the cousin of my own that was killed," McMahon shouted over his shoulder as he carried on with his work.

Turlough and his father started to help, piling goods into the cart.

"I hear tell that our friend Murrough O'Brien committed great slaughter over in Cashel," McMahon said loudly.

"What's that?"

Turlough listened carefully. The name of Murrough O'Brien

had become notorious throughout Munster for the ruthlessness which had earned him his nickname, "Murrough of the Burnings."

"I'm told the people there piled into the church for safety, but he drove his cannonballs through the walls. That must have been slow for him or maybe 'twasn't exciting enough. He piled up turf in ricks against the walls of the church and then set fire to the whole place. He baked them alive, they say: every man, woman, child and priest within." He paused for a moment to stretch his arms. "Baked them the way a woman would bake a cake on a griddle."

In silence they finished helping the McMahons to load their belongings, and then wished them well on their journey to Limerick.

That night Turlough pictured Limerick in his mind. He saw the walls and the narrow streets and he imagined again King John's Castle and St Mary's Cathedral. He remembered the time his father had taken him to the city and they had watched the bull-baiting. When he clenched his eyes shut he could see vividly the dog attacking the bull. The bull kicked it into the air and it fell to the ground with the sound of bones crunching, but leaped to its feet again and went on the attack. Turlough fell asleep with the cruel sounds of the bull-baiting in his ears.

III

A FEW DAYS later they joined a steady stream of people making their way towards the Thomond Bridge across the Shannon into Limerick. None of the groups spoke to its neighbour. It was as if each little knot of people had no wish to be seen by the others.

Turlough walked ahead of his parents, pushing the hand-cart which held their scanty possessions. At the cabin his mother had cast her eyes longingly over what they had had to leave behind. "They'll be here when we come back," his father had assured her. She had given a wan smile and shook her head. Now she walked beside her husband, looking straight ahead.

Bran Óg, bewildered at the crowds of people, trotted quietly beside Turlough.

"It seems every man is on the road these times," his father said bitterly. He clapped Turlough on the shoulder. "You're a clever enough lad, now, but be easy from here on and take care who you speak to," he cautioned.

Turlough narrowed his eyes against the sun. In the distance he could just make out tents with pennants and banners swaying in the air. This was the encampment of Ormond's army, waiting impatiently on the Thomond side of the river for the deliberations between the Confederates and the leaders of the city to come to an end.

The soldiers paid no heed to the refugees making their way to the Thomond Bridge. There, entering the tower on the bridge, a guard looked them over sourly and waved them through. As they crossed the bridge Turlough looked up, as he had done the last time when crossing at this spot; the battlements of King John's Castle towered overhead. But something was different: the battlements and towers were lined with soldiers and a strange flag was flying above the others.

Turlough tugged his father's arm and pointed.

"Aye," his father nodded. "That's the flag of his Holiness the Pope."

"Is he here?"

His father laughed. "No. He's safe in Rome. But Rinuccini is gone over to talk to him and tell him all about our troubles."

They moved through the narrow bustling streets of the Englishtown on the King's Island. Turlough could pick out the tower of St Mary's Cathedral in the distance. Smaller, but closer to him as he walked by the Castle, was the Priory of the Dominicans. A group of people, including some monks, was gathered around it, talking in hushed tones. His father marched in front, clearing a path for Turlough and the hand-cart through the crowded street. They passed the Tholsel and then Fanning's Castle. Turlough knew the way from here. Soon they would be passing over the Bald Bridge into the Irishtown.

"We'll try the market first," his father said. "Stay close to me."

They wandered through the market, making their way by knots of people, stopping every now and then when his father wanted to make an inquiry. Turlough was starving. It seemed that this stopping and questioning would go on for hours. Suddenly Bran Óg froze, then growled in warning. Turlough looked round and found himself staring into McMahon's grim face.

"Boy," McMahon pushed him to one side. "So you did the wise thing," he sneered to Turlough's father and mother.

"It makes more sense for the moment," his father said.

"Peter O'Brien, you were always a stubborn man. Have you a place?"

"No."

"You can come down with us and rest yourselves and get a bite to eat," McMahon said, pushing them in front of him.

He led them through narrow winding streets until they reached a row of small houses. He stopped at one, pushed open the door and disappeared into the darkness within. Turlough stood outside by the hand-cart until his father beckoned him to follow inside. It was a dark little room, badly lit by a weak fire. A sorrowful-looking figure was bent towards the grate; it was Mrs McMahon, staring into the dying ashes. She looked nervously at them.

McMahon waved his hands at his guests. "We might have a bit to eat," he said to his wife and she set about making a meal of soda cake and buttermilk.

Turlough attacked the food without ceremony and passed some to Bran Óg who devoured his portion in one gulp, and then sat, banging his tail off the floor, waiting in vain for more. Turlough wiped the remains of crumbs and buttermilk from his mouth and began to listen carefully to his father and McMahon speaking.

"You might have come at a bad time," McMahon was saying. "I hear stories of a plague."

"I heard that was in Galway," Turlough's father said.

"Well, the stories I hear say it's in Limerick now," McMahon insisted.

"What else is there to tell?" Turlough's father asked, looking anxiously at his wife.

"I'd say they'll be making all the men able to fight put themselves at the disposal of O'Neill," McMahon said. "They'll be looking out for men the likes of yourself." He leaned forward. "'Tis said Cromwell himself is landed," he whispered hoarsely. He looked sharply at Turlough. "Indeed, I saw lads in arms not much older than himself. He might get his chance yet."

Cromwell! Turlough had heard his father use that name before. It was a name spoken in hushed, fearful tones. He saw his mother looking over at him.

His father slapped him on the knee. "He'll wait a little while yet, I think," he said to McMahon.

"Where can we stay?" his mother asked practically.

"The place next to this one is empty," McMahon said.

"We can't move into another's property," she protested.

"We've no property of our own," her husband said grimly.

"They'll have no need of the place next to us," said McMahon. His wife made the Sign of the Cross.

"Lord have mercy on them," Turlough's mother muttered.

"We might have been better where we were than putting ourselves in the way of disease," said his father.

"Would you?" McMahon snorted. "Maybe you'd sooner take your chances with Ironside soldiers burning and looting their way down through Clare than to be behind the walls of this place?"

"God help us all." It was the first words McMahon's wife had uttered.

"The house is there anyway, and no one else in it. My cousin is left from this place and told me to stay as long as I like. I think they'll close off the gates one of these days. Those that are in can take their chances and those that are on the outside will have to shift for themselves. At least we have an army here."

They moved into the house beside the McMahons.

During his first few days in the city Turlough explored the Irishtown quarter. He saw soldiers swagger through the narrow streets, and saw people make way for them. He spent some time in the market, listening to the shouted exchanges of friends and the constant search for gossip between strangers. There were so many conflicting versions of what was supposed to be happening, he realised, that no one knew anything for sure. At the house his father and McMahon exchanged their views of the situation, and here, too, was only confusion.

As the days stretched on, their lives settled into an uneasy pattern. His father had attached himself to O'Neill's army in defence of Limerick and he spent most of his time away from home. He cautioned Turlough not to cross into the Englishtown. But by now Turlough had walked every inch of the Irishtown and he felt tired of its confines. He could look across the Abbey river to St Mary's Cathedral, the turret of Fanning's Castle and the towers of King John's, centre of Hugh Dubh O'Neill's command. Over there, he thought, surely there were people who knew what was going on? So he made his decision. Even at the risk of being accosted by his father on the forbidden territory, he would cross the Abbey river into the Englishtown.

Turlough felt a pang of guilt at his deception. His mother did not look well now; she had become very pale and drawn. Her hair hung in streels where once it had been arranged to suit the shape of her face. But even if he stayed with her, he reasoned, it would make no difference. Anyway, she spent most of her time talking with Mrs McMahon. Although they had been neighbours at Coonagh, they had never been friends; but now, in a city of strangers, they had only each other.

A day or two later he spotted a group of soldiers making for the bridge to cross into the English section. They were followed by a straggle of civilians with children. Turlough saw his chance to get across without attracting attention and he stepped quickly in among them. With his heart beating against his chest, he walked as casually as he could among the soldiers. He studied their uniforms and weapons. But he felt too nervous to stay for long and soon he made his way home, satisfied that he had at least seen a new part of the city.

He went back the next day and stayed longer. Some soldiers noticed his presence, but when they asked his business he waved vaguely towards the Castle and said that he was waiting for his father.

"Is he an officer or a soldier?"

Turlough hesitated. Which was the right answer? He took the plunge: "Soldier," he said. They laughed and relaxed.

After a few days moving from one post to another he found that the soldiers accepted him as a daily sight and talked freely while he sat and listened. Turlough was surprised at how easily his presence was taken for granted, and he became a regular visitor around the Exchange and Castle. There was one post in particular that he favoured, a sally-port where he could look out at the Shannon. The soldiers there were so friendly that they shared their rations with him.

He was with them when they heard the news that Colonel Fennell had abandoned Killaloe to Ireton.

"It won't be long now," they assured each other grimly.

Turlough listened. "Long for what?" he asked after a while.

One of the soldiers grunted and looked closely at the knife he was using to carve a piece of forked wood. "The Ironsides. There's nothing to stop them now." He looked at Turlough. He held up the piece of wood and closed one eye as he examined it. "What is this?" he asked. Turlough looked. It was forked but the soldier had shaved it smooth with his knife.

"Can you use it?"

"I can."

"How will you turn it into a weapon? If you can tell me you can have it."

"A pig's gut."

The soldier nodded his approval and threw the piece of wood to him, laughing. "It's yours," he said. "Get your own pig's gut."

Turlough caught it. He felt its smoothness and smelled the freshness of the wood.

"You can use it to fight off the Ironsides when they burst through the walls," the soldier said bitterly. "I think you'd best go home, lad." He looked at Turlough for a moment, then held out his hand. They shook hands. "Until we meet again," he said and gave a wave before he turned away.

Turlough tucked the fork inside his belt. If it was true about the Ironsides, he thought, he might get his chance to join his father in the fighting, but he knew better than to voice such an idea out loud. He could feel his heart racing with excitement.

If he said anything about the Ironsides his parents would want to know where he had come by the information. He kept it to himself. At the house he waited impatiently for his father's return; his father always talked after he had eaten. But he had nothing to say about the Ironsides. That night Turlough lay awake, wondering if there was any truth in the soldiers' talk. But if the soldiers at the Castle didn't know what was happening, who did?

The day after his discovery Turlough found his mother watching him closely. He spent the day close to the house with Bran Óg, itching with desire to cross to the Englishtown but unable to escape his mother's eye. It was best to do nothing to heighten her suspicion: Turlough didn't want her to start asking him where he had been on other days, for she always seemed to know when he was holding something back. But that evening when his father returned he was walking with a purposeful briskness that had not been there before. Still he did not speak until he had completed his meal. When he had his pipe lit he cleared his throat. "You might as well know," he said quietly, "Fennell has abandoned Killaloe to the Ironsides."

"What does it mean?" his mother asked.

"There's no defence to keep the Ironsides from Limerick. Scouts say Ireton will be here before morning."

The scouts were wrong. Within an hour, as they sat by the fire, they heard a shot from a cannon. His mother jerked upright and blessed herself. Turlough's temples pounded as his blood raced in anticipation. His father stood, his shadow stretching along the wall to the ceiling.

"Turlough," he said, "you're on guard now. Do you understand?"

"I understand."

"Good." His father smiled. "And no more crossing the river to your friends at the sally-port."

Turlough looked at the ground.

"Stay close to your mother until I return." He put his arms around his wife and kissed her on the cheek. He took up his weapons and his cloak. "Make fast the door behind me," he directed.

Turlough fastened the door. He leaned his head against it and listened to his father's boots as they struck off the street, until the sound disappeared into the distance.

IV

TURLOUGH WOKE in the morning with a start. Without looking around he sensed that his father had not returned. He heard a groan from the far corner of the room. He darted from the bed to his mother's side. She was shaking so hard that the rattling of her teeth was like a spoon banging off a pail. Turlough knelt down beside her and placed his hand on her forehead: it was burning. She had difficulty fixing her fevered eyes on him.

"Mrs McMahon," she gasped.

He ran next door and caught Mrs McMahon by the arm. She did not ask him what was wrong but put down the pot she was holding, blessed herself and followed him back to the house, chanting a prayer under her breath.

She looked at his mother for a moment and shook her head. "We'll find your father," she said. "Let you stay here with her, Turlough, God help her." She caught him by the arm. "Don't you go too close to her. She has the sickness, Lord have pity on her. Stay back from her until your father comes," she instructed. "I'll find him somehow."

She ran out into the street.

Turlough looked down at his mother on her bed. Her mouth moved but no sound came. He knelt by the bed again; he could feel the heat from her body. Her lips were parched. He stood up and filled a crock with water, held up his mother's head and let some water dribble onto her lips. She ran her tongue slowly along her lips and nodded to him.

"I have the sickness now, Turlough." Her breath came in spasms. "They'll take me away soon to the pest-house when your father comes. Listen to me carefully." Her hand grasped his. "You remember what you promised me?"

"The Bay."

For a moment there was a faint trace of a smile on her face, then as quickly it was gone. A small fleck of dried blood was on the left corner of her mouth.

"Mother ..." He started to speak but she silenced him with a grip on his hand. He nodded.

"Good boy. The English will take this town. You heard your father last night. Sooner or later. He knows. I want you to go to my father's people. You promised."

"I will go. Have no fear. I promise."

"The Reek. You remember it all. The mountain and the Bay." Beads of perspiration broke out and rolled down the wrinkles of her forehead. "Mayo is a long way from here. You'll have to make the journey on your own. But you'll be looked after when you reach the Bay of Islands. They'll know you there." She broke off and her eyes turned upwards, looking at the smokey ceiling. "They'll be here for me soon." She let go of his hand.

He looked at her. His every fibre cried out to help her but he was powerless in the face of disease. His chest felt tight with the pain of his helplessness.

She clutched weakly at him again and nodded towards the table. He looked behind him: there was a tiny leather pouch resting on the wooden board.

"Take that," his mother whispered.

He took it from the table and opened it. There was a gleam of silver within. He turned it out of the pouch into his hand. It was a medallion; the letters "O. M." were engraved on it.

"Mind that," she said. "My father had it before me. My people will know it. Keep it by you. Let no one take it away."

They both started as the door swung in. Turlough's father came forward, blinking in the darkness of the room. A soldier stood in the doorway, blocking the light. Another soldier entered and looked around uneasily. Their boots ruffled up the straw. His father put his hand under Turlough's elbow and raised him gently to his feet. The two soldiers stood back.

Peter O'Brien stooped over his wife and ran his hand gently down her face. "Oh Máire, Máire, my beautiful Máire," he murmured.

When he stood up his mouth was set in a thin hard line.

"Say goodbye to your mother, Turlough," he commanded softly and turned away.

"What are you doing?" Turlough cried, looking at the two soldiers. Their faces were turned to the floor.

"Your mother has the sickness," his father said. "Her only hope is to go – to go where people can look after her."

"The pest-house! No one – no one comes back. No one comes back from ..." He broke away as his father tried to touch him. "No, I won't let you go," he shouted to his mother.

"Turlough!" she called out.

His father caught him and held him still. "No, no, lad," he said, "it's her only hope." Turlough tried to struggle free but his father was too strong.

The two soldiers made way as McMahon pushed into the room. He caught Turlough by the arm and took him from his father. McMahon's grip was so tight that Turlough could not move. He watched helplessly as the two soldiers carried his mother, one at her head and the other at her feet, into the street.

The street was empty except for a cart. The soldiers placed the sick woman on the cart; with a ruckle of its timber wheels, it began its journey to the pest-house.

Turlough stood, held fast by McMahon, watching, waiting for his father to tell him what to do.

"Wait till I come back," his father said and set off after the cart.

McMahon waited for a few moments before he released his

grip and walked away. Turlough stood alone in the street and watched the sad procession until it had disappeared.

His father was gone all day. When he returned he was silent. They ate without speaking and sat by the hearth until the ashes were cold.

"It's time for sleep," his father said.

"I won't sleep."

"In time you will."

He lay back and listened to the sound of his father's breathing.

"Turlough," his father said.

"Yes."

"Your mother. She is very sick with the plague."

"Will she die?"

"God only knows that," his father said softly. "I must return to the walls tomorrow and I trust you to stay here."

"I should be with you."

"Maybe you should – and I have need of you. But O'Neill will have none of your age at the fighting, and I must do as I am bid. I am a soldier now and not the master of my own will. Do you understand that?"

"I do."

"Stay by the house until I fix what is to be done."

They spoke no more that night.

Two days later his mother was buried in the pit with the other plague victims. Turlough was not there. His father told him what had happened and he took the news in as though it had happened to someone else. He waited for his own tears to come but they did not. He felt cold in his face; his cheeks were numb. He looked at the daylight and it seemed different. He looked at his father who had nothing to say, who shrugged helplessly and went back to his post in the defence of the city.

Now he found himself on his own most of the time. He made his way from the Irishtown across the river to the Englishtown.

He did not find any of the soldiers from his earlier forays. The soldiers were different and preoccupied, and had no time for talking. Their faces were tired, their eyes dark and hollow from lack of sleep.

Turlough lay in bed and thought about the stories he had heard as he wandered the town. He had seen faces go white with fury and fear at the mention of Drogheda and Wexford. Men, women and children, young and old, had been spitted like pigs, it was said. He heard people speak fearfully of what would happen if Ireton took Limerick. Cromwell will want revenge for Clonmel, they said. Wasn't it Hugh Dubh O'Neill, now commanding at Limerick, who had foiled Cromwell there? And hadn't Ireton said that he would have the head of O'Neill whether Limerick surrendered or not? And there were those who said that it didn't matter anyway, that the plague would finish what Ireton had started.

As the fighting intensified, Turlough witnessed what Ireton did to prisoners. He crept onto the battlements during a lull in the bombardment when a crowd of citizens sought refuge outside the walls, throwing themselves on the Ironsides' mercy. As the plague-stricken people shuffled forward, Ireton's soldiers stood back as if to shield themselves from the sickness.

"Go back!" a voice shouted. But on they went, a tribe of sick and sore.

They were met with musket-butts and whips. They stumbled over one another to escape the whips and guns and to make their way back to the protection of the city walls, harried by the Ironsides.

Then Turlough saw the gibbet. Two corpses dangled from it.

One of Ireton's soldiers seized a girl. She screamed, her face twisted in a grimace of agony. The soldier's face was without expression.

Turlough looked away, and saw the man coming forward. His

height set him towering over the surrounding soldiers and civilians. His dress was dark. His dark skin made him look foreign. The bushy curling hair that fell across his forehead seemed to push his hat back from his lean face. Turlough found himself staring into the face. The eyes were hollows of misery. The long sad face seemed to cast gloom on those around him.

"That's Ireton himself. The devil," a voice on the rampart said.

"Only the devil would own a face like that," someone added.

Now, just as Ireton beckoned the soldier to bring the girl forward, an old man staggered towards them. A soldier about to arrest the old man's progress stopped suddenly when he saw that the man's body was twisted with disease.

The old man fell on his knees. He turned his face to Ireton.

"He wants to take her place, it seems," an officer shouted.

On the rampart they watched silently.

Ireton said something to one of his guards. The soldier stepped forward to the gibbet. He pulled a knife from his scabbard and cut through one of the ropes: the dangling corpse fell to the ground with a thud. The soldier fixed a new noose to the gibbet.

Beside Turlough a woman groaned. Turlough felt the colour drain from his face as a soldier dragged the girl onto the platform and inserted her head through the circle of the rope.

The old man started to move towards Ireton but a soldier lashed out and hit him across the chest with a whip. The girl twisted helplessly on the end of the rope as the old man was beaten back to the wall.

Turlough turned his eyes away.

He did not tell the McMahons or his father what he had seen but he listened as Mrs McMahon told her husband of a wonder that was the talk of the city. A monster had been born to a woman a few streets away. It was a creature with one trunk and two heads growing out of it, she had heard. It was said that the two faces wore completely different expressions: when one laughed, the other cried.

And McMahon told her that there was no hope left for anyone in Clare. It was well that they had seized their chance to move to Limerick when they did. General Ludlow had taken Clare and his soldiers drove the people ahead of them the way wolves drive sheep.

When they were alone his father then told him of a miracle that had been seen. It was said that a light in the shape of a globe arose in the Silver Mines. It was brighter than the moon but not as bright as the sun. The people who had seen it reported that it shone first across the city and then, darkening, it moved over Ireton's camp and died out.

"What does it mean?" Turlough asked.

"They say it means that O'Neill and Limerick will be saved. Ireton will die," his father said.

"Then we'll be saved."

"Maybe," his father said. "Turlough, listen carefully to me." He spoke very slowly. "I was talking to the McMahons. They'll take you in if ..." He paused.

Turlough waited but his father remained silent. "If?" he prompted after a while.

"You saw what happened to your poor mother with the sickness. I have to give my time to defending the walls. We don't know what might happen and we have to be ready for anything. I know you're of an age to look after yourself ... "

"Twelve."

"Aye. Twelve. But I'd like to know you were with someone until I can catch up with you. And if, if anything happens and you find yourself on your own ..."

"The McMahons?" Turlough said quietly.

His father gave him a sad smile, laying his hand on his shoulder. "I'll know where you are. I can find you with them. You're safer with them. But if – for any reason – you find yourself alone and you have to leave, go to McNamara of Garykennedy. You know where it is on Lough Derg. Do you remember fishing?" He stopped.

Turlough nodded.

"Do you remember? Ask for McNamara the Boatman. Tell him who you are. Tell him you're my son and he'll look to you. He'll put you on the road that will best take you to your mother's people, Lord have mercy on her soul."

Turlough nodded again. His throat was burning.

His father rifled through the pockets of his coat and extracted a coin. He held it up in front of Turlough who saw that it was not a coin but a silver circle containing a representation of an anchor.

"A seaman's friend," his father said. "Keep it with your mother's medallion."

His father had left when he awoke the next morning. Turlough wandered through the streets. He could not get near the fighting: soldiers pushed him out of the way and told him to get back home.

That evening Ireton launched a fierce, final attack on the city. The battle raged round the walls and battlements. But Ireton had help from within: Colonel Fennel seized St John's Gate, turned the guns against the city and demanded its surrender. His situation hopeless, O'Neill ordered Limerick to open to the Ironsides. Hugh Dubh O'Neill was seized.

In the room Turlough waited with Bran Óg. The sound of fighting rose and fell. "Father will be back soon," he whispered fiercely to the dog. "He will be back." He waited until he was so hungry that he could wait no longer. He gulped his meal and waited again. There was a tremendous bang on the door.

"Father?" he called out.

"Open the door," McMahon's voice roared.

"No."

"Open it, I say." McMahon hit the door so ferocious a blow that it shook.

"It's not to be opened until my father comes."

"You'll be a long time inside then!" said McMahon.

The blood drained from Turlough's face. Not knowing what he was doing he pulled back the wooden guard. McMahon pushed the door open.

"Your father's dead," he said, brushing past Turlough. "No need for the sheep's eyes. He died in the fighting."

"Lord have mercy on him," Mrs McMahon said from the street.

"Where is he?" Turlough asked.

McMahon shrugged. "Buried in a pit I suppose, the same as the rest of them. There's thousands dead between the plague and the fighting. They're burying them as fast as they find the bodies."

"You'll stay with us now, you poor child," Mrs McMahon spoke again.

Turlough shook his head. "I'll stay by myself until it's safe to go the road to Mayo."

McMahon snarled and grabbed him by the arm. "You'll stay with me," he hissed, "and make no mistake about it."

And so he was made to stay with the McMahons. He kept himself out of the way as much as possible. He feared for Bran Óg, too. McMahon regarded the dog darkly, cursing at it and kicking it out of his way. But to Turlough's surprise he never suggested getting rid of it.

McMahon hardly addressed Turlough at all and when he did call out one day "Come with me" Turlough was surprised. He followed silently behind the fat man as he stalked his way through the crowd, all heading in the same direction. Then

Turlough saw what drew them. He watched the hanging of Alderman Fanning, who had been found hiding in the graveyard by Ironsides. And he saw the death of Bishop Terence Albert O'Brien.

"Ireton said there'd be no mercy for that man," McMahon growled at Turlough.

"Why?"

"He was the man that did most to make the city hold out."

"How did Ireton know that?"

McMahon cursed under his breath. He thought for a moment. "Someone must have told him," he said, making a chuckling sound in his throat.

Turlough watched as the bishop stood straight beside the gibbet. When he saw what was about to happen he turned his head away, but McMahon grabbed him by the ear and forced him to stare directly at it.

"There," he whispered hoarsely. "Look on it. That's what comes to them that fight when there's no need of it. There's thousands dead in this city one way or another because some had no more sense than to fight when all was lost."

Turlough walked home in the cold behind McMahon, feeling as though he might never be warm again.

Soon after the hanging of Bishop O'Brien they learned that Ireton had declared that those who wished to leave the city could do so. The McMahons decided that they would leave Limerick and return to Coonagh.

That was Ireton's last decree. He caught the sickness and word swept through the city shortly afterwards that he was dead.

McMahon heaped his goods onto the cart once more. Then, as his wife and Turlough walked behind, he gave the horse a welt of his stick and they made their way for the Englishtown and the bridge over the Shannon.

"It will be good to be back in our own place," Mrs McMahon

said.

"My mother said my place is in Mayo now," Turlough looked at her.

"Did she?" Mrs McMahon's voice quavered.

"And my father said the same."

McMahon brought the horse to a halt. He caught Turlough by the arm and squeezed until Turlough winced.

"You're a liar," he said, "and I'll beat the lies out of you. Your mother said no such thing and your father said you were to be my responsibility and that's the way it'll be. If you try to leave my place without my permission I'll cut the legs off you with this," he hissed, waving his blackthorn stick in front of Turlough's face. "Now, get on with you and mind yourself," he shouted and pushed Turlough in front of him.

Turlough walked as if in a daze. He only raised his eyes again for a moment when he realised that they were passing his own old home and then he could barely make out the cabin for the tears which had flooded into his eyes. But despite the tears he remembered the death-bed promise he had given his mother. He fingered the medallion and medal and it was as if his resolve deepened. The picture of the Holy Mountain in his mind was like a beacon drawing him on to safety; neither the plague, the Ironsides nor the McMahons would keep him in Coonagh.

V

FROM THE beginning Turlough was shown his place in the McMahon household. The shed which he shared with Bran Óg was to be his bed and the scraps from the table were to be their food. He was so often hungry that he took every chance he could to steal more to eat. The hours of daylight were for work, and of that there was no shortage, whether in the fields, seeing to fodder for McMahon's few beasts, or looking to the pigs. Always there were his upland fields with their endless stones, a project which had for long been left untended but which McMahon undertook with a vengeance now that he had free labour at hand. Turlough's back had a permanent ache from bending and his hands sometimes resembled raw lumps of meat from handling stones in the bitter cold.

"You'll work hard and repay the food you're getting," McMahon told him with an oath. "Not to mention your mangy cur," he added.

Turlough was expected to do the work of a grown man. When he was not able for it he was given a cuff across the ear or a beating with a stick.

Sometimes Turlough was able to go across to the McInerneys to meet his friend Tomás, or Tomás would come over in the evenings to visit him in the shed. Tomás nearly always brought some simple food with him and they would sit and eat it while they talked. McMahon knew that the McInerneys would enquire if Turlough was unable to call to them at all, but he warned Turlough against telling about the way he was treated. "If there's anything said I'll break your back," he warned. He looked so angry and hateful that Turlough did not doubt that he would carry out his threat.

McMahon warned him, too, not to be found near his old

home. It was heartbreaking to be so close and yet not be able to go there. His family's old cabin lay empty, and his father's boat was idle on the shore. McMahon had taken possession of the boat, of course.

Mrs McMahon tried to help him but she dared not be seen to take his side. Only once did she do so in front of her husband. After a cold morning spent picking stones in a field, Turlough came up to the cabin to warm himself by the fire. His arms tingled with pain. Mrs McMahon settled him by the hearth so that he could dry his clothes.

No sooner had the chill begun to leave his bones than McMahon entered. He glared from his wife across at Turlough.

"What business has he here?" he snarled at her.

"The poor boy is frozen," she said.

"Is he indeed?" He turned to Turlough.

"Get out of here," he hissed furiously. "Get back out to the field and get on with your work instead of sitting there by the fire like a king in his castle."

As he pulled the door behind him, Turlough heard Mrs McMahon say something; her timid voice was drowned by the loud tones of her husband. Turlough shivered. Again he heard the low murmur of Mrs McMahon's voice, cut short as McMahon roared:

"I'll call slavers to take him away if there's any more trouble from him, and I'll feed his cur to the pigs."

Slavers! Turlough's heart beat against his ribs.

Tomás's father had said there were bands of Ironsides roaming the countryside, snatching boys to sell them off to slave merchants. They sold them to places across the seas where black men lived. Black men! Turlough and Tomás had tried to imagine what a man coloured black would look like. Would he be the colour of a black cow or a black horse? Tomás's father had said, too, that the slavers would make a big trade in orphans, there were so many since the wars started in 1641.

Turlough went out to his work in the freezing fields. To keep his heart up he thought of Tomás, and wondered if he might come over later in the night when they could talk.

Tomás was nearly the same height as Turlough but he was much thinner. He had wild spirits; at home and at play he was the centre of any mischief. He tried always to recapture the fun they had enjoyed before Turlough and his family had left for Limerick. He would jump suddenly and wrestle Turlough to the ground if there was nothing else to do. Sometimes Tomás would even wrestle with Bran Óg.

One evening, when Turlough had little to say, Tomás became impatient. He grabbed his friend and threw him onto the straw of the barn.

"Out with it," he said. "What's eating at you?"

Turlough said nothing.

"You're as stubborn as McMahon says you are," Tomás gave him a dig. "Go on, can't you tell me what's bothering you?"

Turlough thought for a moment. "I'll have to get out of this place," he said. "'Tis the only thing for me to do. If I stay here he'll destroy me." He looked up at his friend. "He might sell me to a slaver."

"He'd never do that! Didn't your father give you to him to mind?"

"Mind this." Turlough pulled up the end of his ragged britches. His lower leg was a mass of bruises. "There's minding for you. Is that what my father gave me to him for?"

Tomás cursed softly.

"He's a pagan savage," Turlough said. "I'll leave this place and the sooner the better."

"How can you leave? The country is crawling with Ironsides, my father says. He met a wanderer the other day who said there's parts of the country you'd not recognise any more. He'd seen sights you'd not see outside of hell. I heard him say that myself."

Turlough nodded. He thought of Ireton and Limerick.

"Did he know of Mayo?"

"Where's that?" Tomás asked.

"'Tis to the north of here. My mother's people are there."

Tomás shook his head. "You've no business to go north from what I hear. Anyway, if Mayo is to the north, that's the way McMahon will expect you go. You'd best go the way he won't expect."

"If I stay here, I'll be crippled from a beating or I'll drop from the work. And if I stay, I'll surely be sold if he wants a few shillings. It's too dangerous to stay much longer."

"He'd never sell you. And anyway, what would you do for food?"

"I'll live off the land."

Tomás laughed. "In the winter? Turlough, wait until the spring. You'll be out in the open now and the frost will kill you. In the spring you have some hope."

Turlough thought about what Tomás had said after his friend had gone home. There was a great deal of sense in it: he would have little chance of making his way in cold weather. And how would he travel when the time came?

He closed his eyes and thought. In his mind he pictured the terrain and it was covered with soldiers. Then he saw the river. His father's boat! He opened his eyes and hugged Bran Óg closer. That was his boat, not McMahon's. He could take it wherever he wished. It was his father's legacy, and with it the river was the path to freedom; he could trick McMahon when the time came.

Through the winter Turlough's life continued in loneliness and cold misery. He had to harden his heart against thinking about what life had been like with his family. When he thought of his parents he grew so sore inside that he felt he would break. He remembered the days on the boat with his father on the Shannon; he thought of his mother before the wars, cheerful and bright when they returned from fishing; and he was torn between laughing and crying when he thought of Uncle Seán, luring foxes, hunting in the woodlands, telling stories and roaring with laughter. With those memories he lay face down in the shed, cuddling close to Bran Óg, trying, sometimes in vain, not to cry out against his forlorn existence.

That first Christmas was the worst time. He discovered on the eve that McMahon didn't pay any heed to the feast; nor did he want Turlough to make anything of it either. He did not want Turlough visiting Tomás on the feast-day.

"It's a time for families," he remarked sarcastically. "There's no family here so stay as you are or you'll know about it."

With Bran Óg licking his hand Turlough stood at the door of the shed and looked at the sky. The ground was covered with frost. The stars twinkled in the still, clear night. He looked down towards the Shannon where the stars were reflected in the gentle movement of the river.

Suddenly he could not fight back the memories that came flooding into his head. In his home he used go to bed on this night bursting with curiosity at what might be there for him when he woke up on Christmas morning. There would be something made by either his father or Uncle Seán - lures or snares or traps - and always there was a woollen garment made by his mother. How did she succeed in making it when he wasn't watching? Coming towards Christmas he always watched like a hawk to see what she was preparing, but he never found out. He had never discovered how she hid it either, Christmas after Christmas.

Now, looking across the hills he realised with a start that he knew where the gifts had been kept - in Uncle Seán's house. A grin stole across his face, but within seconds he was fighting against tears. He battled in vain. They pricked his eyes and slowly slipped down his cheeks. Tears burned his face.

Bran Óg whimpered. Turlough ran the back of his hand against his face and listened. The sound of raised voices came from McMahon's house.

He turned his head in the direction of the McInerneys' cabin. He knew from Tomás that over there the children were still up with their parents. They would be telling stories about feast-days of the past, and before they went to bed they would sing together. "Even now?" he had asked Tomás. "With the war?"

"Ah, the war," Tomás had answered. "My father says life goes on. We'll be dead long enough, he says."

Turlough turned into the shed and lay back. The faces of his father and mother floated into his mind. He fought against the images. He sat up.

"I'll never spend another Christmas like this," he vowed.

VI

THE DAYS lengthened as winter deepened. The harsh January weather gave Turlough relief from his unrelenting labours. McMahon left him alone. The fat man spent hours hanging over the half-door looking out at the fields and the river, his face miserable for want of something to do. He would look balefully at the shed, as if thinking out some scheme to make Turlough's idleness less offensive, but for weeks after Christmas there was nothing to do on the land. Even McMahon could not change the weather.

Turlough and Tomás exchanged visits. Turlough was always on his guard when he was at the McInerneys' place lest he say anything that could get back to McMahon. But he discovered one day, just as the winter weather began to ease, that he had better be extra careful. Indeed, he would have to work fast to prevent McInerney from interfering with his plans.

He was with Tomás when his father came out from the cabin and lit his pipe, propping himself up against the gable of the house.

"He's a dour man, McMahon," Tomás's father said without warning, looking straight at Turlough.

Turlough made no answer. This was not the first time McInerney had made reference to McMahon, but usually he gave up when he realised that Turlough had nothing to say in reply.

"It's hard on him, I suppose, himself and the old woman alone there, neither chick nor child until you came along." He puffed on his pipe and waited, watching Turlough through the curling smoke. When Turlough said nothing he spat and said, "He's a rough man but he knows no better. Of course, if his own son had lived he might be easier to live with, I suppose."

Turlough felt a chill on the back of his neck. A son! "I didn't know he had a son," he said.

"Didn't you? He did indeed, Lord have mercy on the poor fellow. He'd – let me see now – he'd be maybe twenty-five or six if he lived. Would that be right? He was ten when he died and that must be fifteen or more years ago. The only child. A little fellow with fair hair all in curls, I remember. 'Twas your own father, God be good to him, that took the young fellow from the river." He pulled for a moment on his pipe. "Tell me, how is herself?"

"She has little to say," Turlough said.

"Aye. That's true enough. She was never the better of it. D'you know, I don't think I've seen her six times in the last six years. She was always a quiet enough creature, the poor woman, but after that ..." His voice died off and he tapped his pipe on the wall. "How do you pull with himself?" he asked.

Turlough shrugged.

"Is he hard with you?"

"No."

"No? I know him. There's no need to make up stories with me – I know him as long as I'm here. Is he hard on you?"

"No."

"If he is, I'll talk to him."

"No. There's no need."

"Has he no room in his house so you have to live in the shed and the weather that's in it?"

"I'd sooner be in the shed."

"Would you? You like your own company, I suppose."

Turlough put his head down. "Aye, I do."

"Then you're a strange lad. Look at my fellow. If he was on his own he'd burst for want of someone to talk to."

"I'm different," Turlough said.

"We're all different. That's the great thing about us – we're all different. But few of us like to be alone all the time."

Turlough turned away from the man's stare.

Tomás's father put his pipe away and called one of his dogs over. "If there's anything, you tell me," he said. He headed across the fields.

"What does he know?" Turlough turned angrily to Tomás, who had not spoken once his father appeared.

"Nothing."

"You told him something."

"Nothing. I told him nothing," Tomás blushed.

"You shouldn't have ..."

"You can't lie to him," Tomás burst out. "He's too quick for that. He's no fool. He knows you're not telling the truth and he's trying to make up his mind what to do about it. And when he makes up his mind he'll be hard to stop."

"But you'll have to stop him," Turlough said.

Tomás looked aghast. "Me? I'll not stop him. He'll turn me into pig-meal!"

Turlough laughed helplessly. "I don't care what he turns you into; I can't have McMahon watching me any closer than he does already. If your father says anything to him, he'll not let me move at all. I won't even be able to come here, and he'll stop you coming down to me."

Tomás put his hand to his mouth. "I never thought of that."

"No, you didn't," Turlough said. "What did you tell him?"

"That night – Christmas night – we were saying the prayers, and my mother, she said special prayers."

"What special prayers?"

"For your father and mother," Tomás said awkwardly. "And for all the dead of Limerick and Clare, I think. She was calling out names for half the night. When we finished the prayers, she said we must have you up with us and I said you couldn't come. 'He'll be with the McMahons,' my father said and – I said it without thinking – I said 'He won't,' and my mother said 'Where will he be?' 'In the shed,' I said.

"'That's it,' said my father, 'I'm out to bring him back.' 'Twas all I could do to stop him going down there and then! I told him he'd only get you into trouble. He said there'd be no trouble when he'd finished with McMahon. He's a devil when his temper's up. In the end my mother made him sit down and leave things be. But I'd say he's broody about it since."

"He's not to go. I nearly have my plan worked out."

"What is it?"

Turlough hesitated.

"Keep it to yourself, so, if you don't trust me," Tomás said quickly.

Turlough looked at him.

"My father will not get it from me," Tomás said. Then he smiled sheepishly. "But maybe you're right not to tell me; he might trick it out of me. He's a devil like that." He gave Turlough a foolish grin.

"No, I'd tell you – if I had it worked out fully."

"When will you go?"

"What you said. When the days are warmer and longer."

"Can you stick it until March?"

"I don't know. Times I think I can and times I want to move straight away."

"And how will you go?"

"My father's boat."

"But you'll not get up the river," Tomás said, alarmed.

"Not up. Across. Your idea."

Tomás shook his head. "My idea?"

"Remember what you said: he'll expect me to go north. I won't go that way. I'll go across the river, to Mungret. That's the last place he'll think of."

Tom was still unsure. "He'll see the boat gone."

"And he'll think I've stayed to this side of the river. I tell you, he won't expect me to go across. Anyway," Turlough shrugged his shoulders, "there will be no point in talking about it if your father is going to mess everything up."

He began to walk away. He reached under his jerkin and took out the catapult that he had made. A strip of pig's gut, taut and strong, stretched between the fork of the stick. Ahead of him, near the small barn which held the McInerneys' winter stores, some crows were scrabbling round on the ground. Turlough crouched, picked up a stone, and aimed.

With a flutter of wings the birds squawked hurriedly skyward, but one lay on the earth, twisting. Tomás rushed over with Bran Óg at his heels and lifted the clump of black feathers. "Got him!" he called excitedly.

Turlough caught his breath: his aim was getting better and better. But he felt, too, an unexpected melancholy at the sight of the dead bird.

Now he thought about his escape all the time. At night he lay awake, and in his mind's eye he saw his boat moving slowly across the river. It must be at night, he knew, to give him as many hours head-start as possible. And to get the chance to slip away unnoticed. It was McMahon's custom to go to bed soon after his supper as he always rose at first light. What would he say when he discovered Turlough's escape? What would he do? Turlough smiled to himself as he visualised the fat man jumping up and down with rage. He could almost hear the oaths and curses that would come out of his foul mouth.

Tomás didn't ask him any more about his plans but as February slipped away Turlough knew that his friend was waiting impatiently for word. Turlough kept his thoughts to himself. He wanted to be sure that he had worked everything out first. If he made a mistake which destroyed his getaway, he knew that there would not be another opportunity.

He saw less of Tomás now anyway because by March all the McInerneys were attending to the work in their own fields or helping with the fishing. Wary of McInerney's eye, Turlough felt that it would be foolish to risk everything by telling Tomás when he was going to go. At the same time, he missed his friend and the fun they had had together.

With March Turlough's work became harder, too. The muscles in his arms and legs felt as hard as the rocks he lifted in the fields. His back and shoulders had broadened. There were times when he could feel the new strength that coursed through him, but he knew that if McMahon worked him for the coming summer as he had for the winter, his body could well be broken before the year was out.

On the evening that he decided the time had come he took the wallet containing his mother's medallion and his father's silver coin, attached two thin leather thongs to it, and tied them around his waist; the wallet nestled in the small of his back. Putting his catapult into his pocket, he walked with Bran Óg to McInerneys. There were still a few hours to darkness. When Tomás came out they walked to the river.

Tomás had a satchel around his waist. "Food," he said.

"The rabbits will be out soon," Turlough said.

"The mighty hunter," Tomás said jokingly. "Would you pick off a rabbit with the catapult?"

"Why not?"

"They're fast."

"So am I."

They followed the track to the river, speaking little. Turlough wanted to say so much, but he could not bring himself to speak the words. They watched the Shannon flow by. Bran Óg and one of McInerneys' dogs threshed around on the river-bank.

"He's put my father's boat back on the water," Turlough said eventually.

"It's nearly time so."

Turlough looked into his friend's eyes. "It's time," he said. "It's time for me to go home."

"Take this," Tomás said, undoing the leather strap of the satchel around his waist.

"No. Keep it, it's yours," Turlough said.

"Take it. You'll need it."

Turlough looked away.

"Take care," Tomás said quietly. He touched Turlough on the shoulder, and ran back towards his home.

Turlough looked into the flowing waters and felt cold. He shivered. When he looked around he was on his own.

He went back to McMahon's. Darkness was falling now; they would be in bed. He stayed at the shed door and watched the house so that there should be no mistake. All was stillness except for a dog howling in the distance.

He looked around at his miserable surroundings. There was nothing here to take with him. He opened the satchel Tomás had given him. There was a lump of ham and a side of soda-cake. He felt inside. His fingers closed around cold steel. A knife! He searched some more. He took out another object. Flint! He smiled. There had been no need for friends to talk.

Beckoning Bran Óg he made his way slowly to the Shannon. He could hear the river chattering as he got closer. His father's boat bobbed along the shore. He knew where the oars were concealed in the ditch; he took them down one at a time and fitted them in the rowlocks. He boarded and softly called Bran Óg aboard. Bran Óg hesitated for a moment, then jumped.

With a sigh of satisfaction Turlough let out the oars and pulled hard on them. The boat went out into the current.

His journey had started!

VII

HE SAID a prayer of thanks for the light. There were clouds, but the stars and moon provided enough illumination. He could make out the river-bank on the other side; after that he would have to trust to his judgment.

He quickly had his first shock. The current was much stronger than he had imagined when looking at it from the shore. All the power of his muscles went into controlling the oars. Despite his predicament, Turlough grinned at the thought that he had McMahon to thank for the muscles to force the boat to his bidding. He pulled in long, determined strokes, leaning on the oars. But, as the water flowed in a heavy stream beneath him, the strain began to tell on his arms and back.

Turlough's heart beat faster. If he lost control now the river would take the boat from him and do with it as it willed. Perspiration streamed down his back. The river, once friend, now loomed as a powerful enemy. With each lift of the oars he thought his arms would be torn from him. It was taking all his strength to stay in charge. He must not lose control. The splash of the water was like a demon's laughter teasing him as he watched the misty landscape on the opposite side whirling past. Turlough had already been taken beyond the point where he had meant to land. He thought with horror of being swept out the river estuary into the ocean. His father had a story of a fisherman to whom such a thing had happened: he had never been heard of again.

But now the current eased. Turlough rested on his oars for a moment and looked over the side. He had been pushed into the shallows. He let the boat drift parallel to the bank, now that he knew it was within reach, and threw his head back to ease the pain across the base of his neck and his shoulders. He let go of his breath: for the moment he was out of danger.

As Turlough bent to pick up the oars, Bran Óg stuck his head forward and licked his face. It was assurance that the danger was past. Turlough smiled, and began to row slowly for the bank where a low headland jutted into the river. The boat came up against it with a crunch.

"Jump!" he shouted to Bran Óg.

They landed together on the shore. Turlough looked back. The boat was held against the headland. He leaned against it, pushing it out into the shallows. It drifted lazily downward then moved out until the current caught hold of it, gathering speed. Held in the grip of the river, the boat quickly drifted out of sight.

No one would be able to tell where he had come ashore.

Turlough looked around. He had to decide which direction to take. He knew that he had been taken too far downriver, so his best course was to move up along the bank. It would be a long time before light dawned.

He walked along the river-bank. In the darkness he stumbled over a hidden stone and nearly pitched forward into the river. But away from the river the underbrush made it impossible to walk. Turlough moved slowly, with Bran Óg picking his way behind, quiet and not so foot-sure in this strange terrain.

Darkness gave way slowly to dawn and they made better progress. As the sky lightened Turlough moved away from the river to see if he could find his bearings.

After a while he stopped and sniffed. Bran Óg looked around curiously. They were at the bottom of a field which sloped towards a hill. The acrid smell of carrion was carried on the air. Turlough moved slowly forward towards a ditch at the top of the hill. The smell became stronger. He held his nose. Two rotting cattle were heaped in the ditch.

He looked across the fields. In the distance he spied the

arched gable of a church. They made their way to it.

As he came closer he saw that the church had been put to fire, but much of the roof was still intact and they could shelter beneath it. He crept slowly in and began to explore the ruin. Through a crumbling window he saw a little graveyard at the back, all overgrown. Weeds and briars shook gently in the wind.

He sank back against a wall, and Bran Óg stretched out beside him. All he wanted to do was fall into a deep sleep. He fought against it but his eyelids drooped, and within moments he had fallen into a world of darkness.

From the depths of sleep barking hauled him back into wakefulness. He sat up with a groan. His back screamed for ease; his limbs were stiff and his body pierced with cold. He looked around in confusion and then saw Bran Óg shivering as he stood on guard looking towards the ruined doorway of the church.

It was becoming dark again. He had slept most of the day! He felt lost.

The sound of voices in the distance carried in the stillness of the evening. Turlough winced with the pain in the back of his legs as he stood upright. He moved with effort towards the doorway. He listened, shushing Bran Óg as the dog began to growl. Still the voices came on and then suddenly they stopped.

Turlough peered round the doorway, his eyes slowly becoming accustomed to the growing gloom.

Something stirred!

Out of the half-light two figures came into focus. One was large, the other small. Panicking, he took the knife from his belt.

He darted back inside the door and looked around for a place of refuge. There was nowhere to hide. It was too late anyway. The figures, each wearing a heavy cloak, filled the doorway.

They stood there, staring at him.

The big man with a greying beard had a woodsman's axe slung inside his belt. Over his shoulder he carried a heavy sack. His small companion had a mop of red hair and as he came forward Turlough saw that he walked with a limp. His thin face was dominated by a long thin nose. His mouth was twisted as if in pain but his face was lit up with lively blue eyes that were at odds with the rest of his appearance. When he came closer Turlough saw that he had a squint in his left eye. He had a coil of rope draped over his shoulders.

"What do you do here, boy?" the taller one boomed at Turlough.

The smaller man limped forward. He closed his left eye for a moment, staring in an odd manner at Turlough.

Bran Óg stirred uneasily, his hackles rising.

"If that brute moves, you are both dead," the big man said, drawing the axe from his belt.

Turlough wrapped his arms around Bran Óg and waited. He tightened his grip on the knife, keeping it down by his side.

"What are you doing here, boy?" the small one repeated. His voice was light but cracked with hoarseness.

The big one towered over Turlough and Bran Óg. The axe in his hands shone. He put his sack on the ground. It hit the earth with a clank of metal.

"Is that brute safe?" asked the small man as he came forward.

"He's harmless," Turlough said.

"Are you going to do something with that knife?"

Turlough looked at the knife in his hand.

"Because if you're not you'd best put it back down."

Turlough tightened his grip on the knife. He looked from one to the other. He put the knife back in his belt.

The big man looked at him sourly. "Where are you from?"

Turlough pointed in the direction of the river.

"Why are you here in this place?" the smaller man circled round Turlough.

"I was hunting."

"Were you now?" he said. "Haven't you the great eyes to be hunting in the dark?"

"Hasn't he?" The big one was standing on what had once been an altar, the axe in his hand glinting in the faint light.

"'Tisn't dark long," Turlough spoke up.

"True enough," said the small one. "But these are dangerous times to be out in the dark, alone." He picked up Turlough's leather pouch, examined it, then drew out a piece of soda cake. "How long were you planning to stay out for?" His eyes seemed so piercing Turlough felt that the man could see what he was thinking.

"His name is Shane," shouted the big man at Turlough.

"And his name is Murty. What might yours be?"

"Turlough."

"I see," Shane said. He closed his left eye again and looked Turlough up and down. "What age would you be?"

"Twelve."

"Are you now. A big lad for your age. You're as big as myself. And it's a long time since you were twelve," Murty shouted over at him.

"And where would your father be?" Shane asked.

"Dead, is it?" said Murty.

"Did he die of the plague?" Shane added. "I hear a fright of people died of the plague down Limerick way."

"In Limerick," Turlough said.

"Fighting?" Shane's voice rose hoarsely.

"Fighting."

"And your mother?" Shane asked.

"The sickness."

"You're all alone so?" Shane said.

Turlough shrank back from him. Bran Óg started to growl.

"Shut that dog up, boy," Shane said quietly.

"Easy, Bran," Turlough warned the dog.

"There's no need to fear the two of us. Are you hungry?" Shane asked. "There's a remedy for that." He picked up Turlough's pouch. "I don't know," he muttered. "A big young fellow like you would eat the side off a pig and there's no more here than bread and a bit of salted pork. And do you see himself beyond there?" he asked, pointing over at his big companion. "I saw the day that man would eat a young calf all by himself and not a bit left over for anyone."

Murty rifled through his sack and drew out a lump of thick grass. He held it in one hand while with the other he undid the bundle to reveal an egg nestling in the centre of it.

"Take it, young fellow. 'Tis good for what ails you."

"There's nothing wrong with me," Turlough said. He looked doubtfully at the egg.

"Give it here." Shane took a straw from his belt. He screwed his eyes up in concentration and stuck his tongue out. Under the gaze of Murty and Turlough he carefully inserted the straw into the egg. "Suck away on that," he said, handing the egg to Turlough.

"I like a bit of meat myself," Murty said to one in particular.

"The devil mend you, then," Shane retorted. "You never have enough to eat no matter how much you get."

"You're cold, boy," Murty said. "You look like someone came from the river."

Turlough looked down at the mud covering his clothes.

"We'd better heat you up before you die on us." He disappeared out of the building and returned within a few minutes with sticks for making a fire. The other two watched while he bustled about making the fire which was soon blazing comfortably within the ruins.

As the warmth went through his body Turlough felt the life returning to his perished limbs. The fire and the warmth of Bran Óg lying against him made him feel drowsy. He closed his eyes but fought against sleep. Behind closed eyelids, he had to stay awake. He heard the men murmuring for what seemed like hours but he could not make out what they were talking about. His eyelids grew heavier. Just as he was about to yield to exhaustion, Turlough saw out of the corner of his eye that Murty was throwing more wood on the fire. He shook himself. He pinched himself on the leg as hard as he could bear. The murmurs of the two men died away. After a while their snores told him that they had fallen asleep.

Turlough eased himself into a sitting position. He beckoned Bran Óg. They slipped away from the fire, outside the ruined church into the cold. The night seemed black as pitch after the glow within. He groped his way along, then suddenly bumped into a huge shape. His heart thumping wildly he stretched his hand forward. He felt the warmth of a body and then with relief realised that he had bumped into a horse.

Bran Óg barked softly. Turlough turned. He was grabbed by an arm from the blackness.

"Aren't you the scheming brat," Murty hissed. He held Turlough by the shoulder in a grip of iron. With his other hand he deftly slipped the knife from Turlough's belt.

The limping figure of Shane appeared beside him. "That's the end of you, boy," he croaked. "You'll be dead the next time you try any more of them tricks. And you'd best quiet that beast or he'll feed the crows."

They pushed him back into the ruins.

"A crafty one," Murty said.

"I'll give him 'crafty' if he tries the like of that again," said Shane. "And he'll get 'crafty' tomorrow when we put him up for sale to our friend," he chuckled.

VIII

THE PAIN from the tightness of the ropes binding his arms allowed only fitful sleep. Turlough was comforted only by the warmth of Bran Óg. All night the ruined building echoed to the hoarse snores of his captors. By morning Turlough was racked with chills; his legs and arms were so numb he could not get himself into a sitting position.

Murty came to life first. He stood up and stretched, clapping his hand loudly across his belly. He shoved his foot into Shane's back and brought him out of his sleep.

Glumly, they ate from the food in Murty's sack.

"I suppose we'd best feed our friend here?" Murty suggested halfheartedly.

"He'll not eat with his hands behind his back," Shane observed.

Murty undid the ropes around Turlough's hands, but left his ankles bound. Turlough snatched up a piece of cake and ate it greedily. It was hard and dry, and tasted musty. When he had taken the edge off his hunger he gave some to Bran Óg. The dog eyed the bread doubtfully, sniffed at it for a while, but in the end swallowed it.

They were soon ready to move. Murty tied a leash around Turlough's waist, undid the rope around his ankles, and led him to a sad-looking piebald pony which waited in the graveyard, its front legs hobbled. Murty passed the leash to Shane, who had mounted his horse, and then he stooped to pick up stones from the ground before turning on Bran Óg.

"You mangy mongrel, we'll not be taking you along." And he threw large stones at the barking dog.

"Run, Bran Óg, run!" shouted Turlough. And he did, scampering off into the shelter of nearby trees with a yelp.

They began their journey, Turlough more worried about what would become of Bran Óg than about himself. Murty took the lead on foot, covering the ground with great lengthy paces until he was soon a considerable distance ahead of the other two. Turlough's pony hobbled along; he was made to keep just ahead of Shane.

The journey seemed to go on forever, but at last they were within sight of the gates of the city. Murty halted and waited for them to catch up.

"We'd best untie him so there'll be no questions asked," he said to Shane.

Murty undid the rope. Then he caught Turlough by the throat.

"One word out of you, boy, to anybody ..." he glared at him. "Do you hear?"

Turlough nodded, gasping for breath.

"I'll squash your head in like a beetle," Murty spat, releasing his grip. He turned back to Shane. "Whoever we meet, I'll do the talking."

They entered the gate without any trouble. Just inside the wall Turlough saw a gibbet. Murty caught him by the shoulder and hissed into his ear, "See where a good man might end up, boy."

The three of them stood looking at the empty gibbet. Turlough turned to look at the tower. It carried an inscription. He read it to himself, calling up from memory the Latin he had learned from Fr O'Dwyer.

CARLO REGE
REGNANTE
PETRO CREAGH
PRETORE
ANNO DOMINI 1643.

His lips moved silently as he slowly read through it, making his translation: "King Charles Reigning, Peter Creagh, Mayor, the Year of Our Lord 1643."

Murty pushed him in the back and they moved forward into the Milk Market. It was packed with traders.

"I could sell the thirst on me," Shane said, throwing Murty a coin.

Turlough looked around while they waited for Murty to return with the milk. He saw that behind him a man, dressed in the Irish fashion, leaned against a wall. A straw between his teeth, he looked coolly towards Shane. He was of average height, lithely built, with a lean weather-beaten face. There was a slight scar, a short white line visible above his left eyebrow. Shane suddenly looked around, as though he sensed he was being examined, and scowled at the stranger.

Murty returned with three mugs spilling over with milk. Turlough took his gratefully and let the cool liquid spill down his throat.

"Men."

Turlough looked up. The stranger had come forward and was grinning at Murty and Shane. They looked at him with distrust.

"I'm in the market for horses," he said, clapping the piebald across the withers. "Or anything else that might be going."

"We've nothing for sale here," Murty answered.

"Maybe not horses, then."

"No horses," Murty snarled.

"Indeed so. But I'm not confined to horses."

"We've nothing for sale," Shane said impatiently.

"'Tis easy enough to make money these times if you know what's for sale," the stranger said.

"What does that mean?" Murty asked.

"What it says."

"Speak straight, man, and come out with what you want to say," Murty snapped.

"There's men looking for boys to sell abroad," the stranger said. "Good money on offer."

"Sell our own brother!" Shane exclaimed.

"Sell our own flesh and blood?" said Murty, throwing his arm around Turlough's shoulders.

"I'd be off out of here, if I was you, my friend, before I tell these decent people what you are after saying," Shane said, squinting at the stranger.

"You'll be torn limb from limb," Murty raised his voice.

"An honest mistake, my friends," the stranger said. "I'll bid you good day." He made them a slight bow and sauntered off.

Murty pulled the mug from Turlough's hand and caught the one Shane tossed to him. He poured the dregs onto the cobblestones and brought the mugs back to the milk-seller.

"Move on," Murty ordered as soon as he came back, pushing Turlough forward. "I didn't like that," he said over his shoulder to Shane.

"Pay no mind," Shane said. "There's plenty trying to make a living buying and selling. Aren't we doing it ourselves? Sure you don't like strangers. You never did. The size of you and you don't like strangers," he laughed to himself.

They made their way slowly through the twisting streets and stopped outside a little cabin. Murty rapped quickly on the door. There was a shuffling inside, followed by the sound of iron on iron before the door swung open. Murty hustled Turlough inside. The door slammed shut behind them. Shane was left outside.

Turlough had to adjust to the gloom. The room was lit only by a small candle. It smelled of grease and dirty straw littered the floor. The one who opened the door was a very small, stocky man with a large head. He had no neck, it seemed, and the only hair adorning his head came from a straggly beard which rested on his chest.

"Uncle Peadar," Murty said cheerfully, but the bald man ignored him and stared stonily at Turlough.

As his eyes became accustomed to the shadow Turlough made out the figure of an ancient woman covered in a shawl, sitting by the hearth. She stared sightlessly at them from a pair of unblinking yellow eyes. She made no movement except when she raised a cracked mug to her lips and gulped its contents noisily.

"Who's this?" Peadar spoke. For such a heavily-built man he had a surprisingly light voice.

"A prize we picked up."

"Prize indeed."

"The others?"

Peadar jerked his head towards the ceiling. "Sound as lambs in a pen."

There was a bang at the door. Peadar opened it and admitted Shane.

"Uncle," Shane gave greeting, to which Peadar made no reply. "And how's herself?" he asked, nodding over at the old woman by the hearth.

"She'll be none the better of you anyway," Peadar said curtly.

"No change there then," Shane said, pulling rope from his satchel. "You," he barked at Turlough.

Murty caught Turlough by the shoulder and hurled him over to Shane.

"Put your hands behind your back," Shane ordered. He bound Turlough's hands tightly. "Put him with the others," he ordered Murty.

Turlough was pushed forward up the narrow wooden stairs until he reached a padlocked door.

"Key!" Murty shouted down.

There was shuffling downstairs and then Peadar came panting up to them. He threw the key to Murty who unlocked the door and forced Turlough forward. The door slammed as he fell face down onto foul-smelling straw.

"Another one in the stew," a boy's voice said.

Turlough picked himself off the ground. Very close to him a figure lay slumped against the wall. It was a boy. He was dressed in rags. His pale face gleamed in the darkness.

"Have you a name?" a second voice asked.

Turlough twisted. Under a boarded-up window sat a boy some years older than himself, perhaps sixteen. In the thin ray of light breaking through a crack in the board Turlough could make out freckles and a mop of curling red hair.

"You'll be lodging here for the night," the boy said. "But it won't cost you much. You might as well rest your bones anyway." He gave a short bitter laugh.

A racking cough rent the room. Turlough, startled, saw a slight, thin body stretched on the straw. His face, thin and pinched, was turned towards Turlough. His cheeks were two bright red patches under the dark hollows of his eyes.

"We think he's dying," the bigger boy said.

Turlough slumped down. There was a sick, hollow feeling in the pit of his stomach. "How long are you here?" he asked finally.

"Three days."

"Who are you?" the bigger boy asked.

"Turlough O'Brien."

"He's Brian," the boy said. "I'm David. The little fellow's Risteard. We think he has the sickness."

They were silent for a moment, looking over at the sunken body of Risteard.

"How did they catch you?" David asked after a while.

They listened carefully to his story.

"They're a cute pair of wolves," David said when Turlough had finished. "They *are* just like wolves. They stole me away from my mother the way a wolf will make off with a lamb. She met them in a neighbour's house and they supping on spuds and buttermilk. They said they were dealing in cattle, but they did no deal there even after they were fed. My mother told them the way we were, my father dead and I the oldest. They said they knew a place for a cow-herd and the long and the short of it is we agreed I should go with them." His voiced trembled. "And this is where they brought me."

"What do they want us for?" Turlough asked.

"I think – I think they're keeping us to sell for slaves," Brian said.

Trying to keep his voice steady Turlough asked, "Do you think it's true?"

"'Tis true," David said sharply. "The Ironsides is selling lads to be shipped to the other end of the world."

"To where?"

"I don't know. But it's to the other end of the world, I heard tell. I've heard them two talking when we were on our way to this place." David paused for a moment. "There's men with ships to sail over the world. And there's men with places on the other side of the world looking for the likes of us to work it."

They fell silent. Again a harsh cough sounded from the straw. Turlough looked; Risteard's body lay quivering with fever. When the small boy had settled back into an uneasy sleep Turlough looked over at Brian.

"How did you come here?" he asked.

Brian shook his head. "The one with no neck caught me," he said. "I was like a dog you'd see scratching around for scraps. I'd move around from cabin to cabin and each one would throw me some bit to eat, and a place to lie down. Those wolves below must have been watching me all the time. The one with no neck found me one night I had no place and told me he'd give me a bed and a bit to eat and – and that was it. They had me and here I landed."

"Shush," David said hoarsely. He had heard a footstep.

A key turned and the door swung outwards. It was Murty. The light from a candle he held threw flickering shadows onto the wall.

"Quiet night, boys," he said loudly. "I'm afraid we've no visitors for you." He came across the floor, stepping by Turlough, and stood over Risteard.

"Any stir out of this one?" he asked.

"He's dying," Brian said.

"Is he now? Well, he'd best not." Murty stooped down and felt the little boy's forehead, frowning. He stalked across the room and out the door, leaving it open. "Bring it up," he shouted. He came back into the room and waited until Shane entered with a wooden board held in his two hands. There were four bowls of liquid on the board.

Murty went to each in turn and untied their hands. Then Shane gave each of them a bowl. "What about him?" Shane asked when there was only one bowl left.

"Leave him to God," Murty said darkly. "Now, drink up that gruel, boys. We want you fresh and lively for inspection tomorrow."

"It's a long run to the Barbados, I hear tell," Shane said, "and there'll be many's the night you'll be glad of the bite of supper."

Turlough ate slowly, looking up from the bowl to take in his surroundings in the candlelight. Shane and Murty stood near the doorway. What if they charged their captors? He glanced swiftly around. Neither David nor Brian showed interest in anything except their food. Then David looked up. A frown crossed his face and he stared at Turlough. Very slowly, he shook his head.

Turlough turned back to the food. The liquid mess tasted foul but he forced it down. When he was finished Shane snatched the bowl out of his hand; Murty tied him again.

When the slavers had gone Turlough crawled painfully across

the floor and positioned himself beside Brian, with his back against the wall. They did not speak.

He lay awake for what seemed hours, his mind a turmoil of confused pictures. His bid for freedom had lasted just one day. Now he was a prisoner with a worse fate before him.

The war brought by the English; the terror of the plague; the horrors of Limerick; the misery of his stay with McMahon; all crowded together in his head. He thought he saw his dog running free in the fields outside his old home; it was a dream, a mistake in his mind.

IX

HE WOKE to the sound of Brian's groaning. "My hands are dead," he whispered across to Turlough.

"So are mine," Turlough said, "and my feet too." And they were. The pain was worse than he had felt when he was tied up in Mungret.

They held their breaths at the sound of creaking on the stairs. A key grated in the lock. Murty entered and stood inside the door, looking down at them with his hands on his hips. His eyes were sleepy. Shane followed, bearing the board with the bowls on it. He shuffled across the straw. "They can't eat till you open their ropes," he said to Murty.

Murty undid the ropes roughly. The boys were unable to take hold of the bowls until the blood found its way through their arms and legs. Shane stood over them, cursing under his breath while he waited.

Turlough took the bowl from him, barely able to keep his hands from trembling.

Shane glared down at him. "If that food goes on to the floor you can lick it up, for it's all you get."

Beside him Brian sipped at the liquid in which oatmeal floated in lumps. Then as he swallowed he began to choke. His head banged against Shane's leg. With a curse Shane pulled his leg away and Brian fell forward. His bowl tumbled onto the ground and he watched with a groan as the contents soaked into the straw.

Shane kicked the bowl across the floor. He caught Brian by the hair and yanked him upright. Brian gave a cry of agony and lashed out with his fist. Shane swiped him across the chest and sent him reeling over onto his back. Then, cursing, he strode past Murty and clattered down the stairs.

"We'll have to wake this one up sometime," Murty turned his attention to the boy lying on the floor. He dug his boot into Risteard's side.

The boy stirred, groaning, and then opened his eyes. His face was a deathly pallor.

"Can you eat, boy?" Murty asked.

Risteard shook his head.

"Devil mend you." Murty growled. "Leave down those bowls," he called to the others.

Turlough was suddenly alert. Was there a chance, now that they faced only one man? He felt his foot being nudged. He glanced at David. David's eyes said "no".

"Hands behind backs," Murty ordered. He tied the three of them again, gathered his bowls and left.

"Don't be a fool," David whispered.

Turlough started to protest but Brian cut him short.

"We've all thought of it. But look: there's a bolt on the door below. They'll have us before we even get to the door, let alone get it open. And what do we do with Risteard?"

Turlough nodded.

"You've the right heart," David said, "but it's the wrong time. Wait," he added. "Our time will come."

Turlough could not tell how much later it was when they heard a banging on the door. The sound of voices, quiet and indistinct, drifted up from below. Shortly they heard the tramp of steps on the stairs.

It was Peadar. He looked at each one for a moment, his large face expressionless. It was as if they were specimens of animals in which he had an interest.

"Watch this," he said suddenly.

He held up his hand and they saw that he was holding a horseshoe. He caught the ends of the horseshoe in each hand and began to force it open. His lips parted and he gritted two rows of perfectly formed teeth. His breath began to come in quick, sharp snorts. Slowly the horseshoe began to bend.

The boys' eyes widened in wonder. Each one moved his gaze from the hands to the short hairy arms, with biceps bulging as the horseshoe became almost a straight length of iron. Each of them felt as if his heart had stopped beating and that the only sound in the room came from Peadar. It seemed to Turlough that this small, bull-like man was a magician. A magician of evil.

Peadar held the horseshoe in front of them. "I could do that to your arm," he said, "if you move at the wrong time." He threw it to the floor.

He untied the ropes on Brian and pulled the boy to his feet. Pushing him across the floor, he nodded to the doorway. He untied David and then Turlough. Finally he stood over Risteard and shook his head. "He won't even earn the price of his feeding," he said, pointing Turlough and David to the door.

They were unsure of their footing after being bound for so long. Each placed a hand against the wall as he made his way cautiously down the stairs, Peadar following behind. At the bottom of the stairs he pushed them into the room where Murty and Shane stood by the window.

In the centre of the room stood a large fat man. His face was weather-beaten, and his rich fancy clothing hung uncomfortably on his huge frame. Blinking in the light, Turlough saw that the man had thick heavy rings on both hands.

This stranger subjected Turlough to the coldest stare he had ever imagined could belong to a human being. The eyes were like those of a hunting animal. Turlough held the hard preying eyes, then turned away. The man smiled shortly. "Come here," he said.

Turlough crossed the floor silently, as if in a trance. The stranger hovered round him, then reached out and felt the muscles on his arms.

"Well?" Murty broke the silence.

"Tonight," the stranger snapped and turned away from the boy.

Murty and Shane followed him to the door.

"Back up the stairs," Peadar ordered.

Within minutes they were back lying on the straw with their hands bound again. Each remained silent with his fears as darkness drew down.

They were startled when a bang on the door downstairs reverberated through the house. There was the sound of scrambling below and of the shutter on the inside of the front door being drawn. Voices were raised. Then there was a yell and a crash as wood broke. The yelling grew louder.

Heavy blows shuddered their door. They watched with a mixture of fear and fascination as it slowly gave way. Through its remains came a sword, followed by a bearded face.

Turlough gasped. It was the man from the Milk Market who had accosted Murty and Shane. Gliding across the floor he slit their bindings with his sword.

"Out you go," he ordered.

"Him," Brian said, pointing to Risteard. "He can't move."

"Out!" the man roared.

They scrambled down the stairs. Inside the front door Peadar lay on the floor. His face was covered by a foolish grin as though he had recognised a joke on himself. His chest rose and fell, panting. His closed eyes seemed odd against the foolish smile on his face.

Shane was slowly sinking to the ground, felled by a blow to the back of his neck. Then he lay prone on his face. The old woman by the fire stared sightlessly around the room.

Murty was holding off three men with the aid of a short wooden staff. It had been much longer but was being systematically reduced by a sword in the hand of one of the attackers.

One of the men attempted to move to the big man's rear but received a blow to the arm which sent him flying backwards on top of Turlough.

"Out, boy, out," he shouted at Turlough and pushed him to the front door.

The three boys tumbled out of the door into the darkness of the street, gulping at the fresh clean air, and were swept along the street by their panting rescuers.

X

WITHIN MINUTES they were in the shadow of the Dominican church, their backs against the wall as they waited. The leader of the rescuers was speaking to a man who held Risteard in his arms.

"Who is he?" Turlough whispered to the man beside him.

"He's Eamon O'Riain from Cragg, a few miles out."

"Why is he doing this?"

"He hates slavers. They killed his young brother a while before Christmas. He'll swing for them if he has to."

He heard Brian asking, "How are we to get out of here?"

"Leave that to us," a deep voice grumbled. "Keep your mouths shut. There'll be plenty of time to talk when we leave Limerick behind us."

The men nearest the corner of the wall had their swords unsheathed. They moved out from the wall, their weapons at the ready. Turlough and the others watched them. Now he held his breath, too, as he heard a noise approaching from the other side of the wall. It was a hoarse snuffling. He closed his eyes: he knew the sound. The men with the drawn swords stood at the ready. Turlough held his breath and waited for the conflict to start. Instead he heard light laughter. He looked to the corner, barely restraining himself from a hoot of delight.

Bran Óg's face was peering round at him. He looked at the huddled men and the boys, his tail waving in the air. He scampered across to Turlough who caught him up in his arms.

"Is he yours?" the man beside him asked.

"I haven't seen him since Mungret!"

"Mungret! He must have followed you in then and waited. You can't beat a dog for friendship. Best keep him quiet."

Turlough held onto Bran Óg, who quivered with excitement.

O'Riain beckoned his men together. "The gate above is crawling with soldiers," he said. "Between slavers, informers, Ironsides and the devil knows what else, we'll have to be well on our guard. Who counted the patrol?"

A young man said that he had.

"Are you sure you got it right?"

"Aye. Sure enough." His face tightened as he watched the worried expression of O'Riain.

"We'll wait a bit. That patrol seems set to stay at the gate and if you are right they should have moved off by now." He looked anxiously at the sky. "There's too much moon for us to take our chances. We'll have to be very careful in getting out."

"We're not safe here," someone said.

"That patrol might be there because they have information about us."

"Could those slavers have gone to them?"

O'Riain gave a short laugh. "If they moved from the house they must have skulls like rocks. What would they know anyway?"

"I don't think they'll go to the Ironsides," Turlough said.

"Why not, lad?" O'Riain asked.

"They were acting afraid coming in. I wouldn't think they're real slavers. They're just suppliers, I'd say, and they take their chances, too."

"Maybe," a doubtful voice muttered.

"The lad may be right," O'Riain cautioned. "They're just vermin living on whatever they can find." He was silent for a few minutes. "I'll scout out the gate," he said.

"I'll go with you," a man close to Turlough offered.

O'Riain shook his head. "I'll go." With that, he moved quickly away and was gone around the corner. He was gone a very short time. "Something's up," he announced when he came back. "They're ready to move off. But we'll give them a while yet before we move. Let those of you with food share it out before we start the journey for Cragg."

Some of the men produced chunks of oaten cake from little satchels carried around their waists. They broke them up and passed them around among the others. A lump of the cake was thrust into Turlough's fist and he was told to eat it. He had no difficulty obeying the order.

"How is the sick lad?" O'Riain asked.

The man who held Risteard shook his head.

"Is it the sickness?" a voice asked.

"God knows," the man answered.

"No fear of him. The Healer has worked on worse than that," O'Riain said, but Turlough noted that his voice was unsure.

"My belly thought my throat was cut," Turlough's minder chuckled as he shook crumbs from his beard.

They munched without speaking until every crumb of the welcome food had been devoured.

"Where's Cragg?" Turlough asked eventually.

The man pointed north. "We'll follow the river towards Killaloe."

Turlough was unable to quell a surge of excitement. Did he dare to hope that after all his misfortune he would be able to begin his journey for Mayo by getting help from McNamara of nearby Garykennedy? He clutched Bran Óg closer.

"Right," O'Riain said softly. "We'll strike out."

As silently as possible they moved from the shadow of the church. Making his way carefully from the city where he seemed to have known nothing but sorrow, Turlough became conscious of the nocturnal sounds. Distant voices carried on the windless night. From one house came the shrill cry of an infant demanding attention; as they passed another they heard the sound of drunken fighting. On their way past a shabby cabin an alert dog nearly scared them senseless with a sudden snarl. From a brightly-lit building poured raucous singing. The shadows inside the window showed the helmets of soldiers.

They filed swiftly through the unguarded gate and left the city.

Turlough stuck close to Brian and David. All three of them were tired and the brisk walking pace of their rescuers soon had them panting. They gritted their teeth, keeping up with their longer-legged companions, but feeling greater and greater strain on their legs as the journey continued. After a while they lost track of time, walking mindlessly in the midst of their rescuers for hour after hour after hour.

Then, without warning, they stopped. Turlough could feel the men in front holding their breaths, their weapons at the ready.

"Is that yourself, O'Riain?" a voice questioned.

"Ourselves," O'Riain called out, laughing.

"You took your own sweet time."

"Aye, we had a sweet time of it while you stayed scratching yourself in the bushes."

A small thin man with a shock of grey hair, holding a lantern in front of him, appeared out of the bushes. His sharp eyes took in the party and his lips moved as though he was counting the numbers. He took in the sight of the boys without comment.

"Did you bring the dray?" O'Riain asked.

"Over there in the clump."

O'Riain directed the man with Risteard to place the small boy on the dray; then he beckoned the three boys to join him. All three fell into the straw-filled cart as if it had been lined with mattresses of down. Bran Óg jumped up beside Turlough. The boys stretched their limbs and in no time had fallen into a sleep that was assisted by the gentle rolling of the dray as the horse bore them into the hills.

"Down with you, lads," a voice roared from far away.

They came into sitting positions, trying to shake the sleep from their eyes and ears.

"Where are we?" Brian mumbled.

"Cragg, laddie," the big man who had roared them awake shouted. Turlough remembered seeing him during the rescue, a bearded silent presence who had stayed close to O'Riain. "Come down out of that," he said, as he gently caught hold of Risteard and hoisted him down from the cart. Risteard's eyes remained closed.

"Down, lads," O'Riain came over. "Into the cabin there with the lot of you and my mother will fit you up with places more proper for sleeping in."

They stumbled through the darkness to the welcome light of the lantern in the doorway. Turlough felt that he would not stay awake long enough for the woman to find him a place. The tall thin woman looked sharply from one to the other, pointing towards pallets where they were to lie down. He was asleep before his head even reached straw.

XI

THE SUN was high when Turlough woke to the delicious smell of cooking. The scent of bacon hung in the air and over the fire was a black pot bubbling with potatoes. He looked around suspiciously, taking in the sight of his rescued companions and the long thin woman from the night before. He rubbed the sleep from his eyes.

"Good day to you, boy," the woman said.

Turlough nodded to her.

"A fine slugabed you are," she laughed.

He saw that the others were barely able to restrain their laughter. Turlough looked down at himself to see what was amusing them. Had he all his clothes on? Then, with a shock, he realised that Risteard was sitting up with Brian and David. There was a liveliness in his dark eyes and the glowing red was gone from his cheeks.

"Eamon took him to the Healer," Brian said.

"And he laid his hands on my head and my ears ..." Risteard said, "and then he took out my tooth."

"And by noon the sickness was gone," David blurted out.

"By noon?" Turlough said, unable to keep up. He looked to the window and saw the cloudless sky.

"'Twas a rotten tooth he had," David said.

"Tooth?"

"Show him," Brian directed Risteard.

Risteard took the tooth from his pocket and placed it on the table. "Isn't it small enough to have caused so much misery," he laughed shyly.

They enjoyed themselves at Cragg. They were made to feel so comfortable that within a few days it was as if they had always known O'Riain and his followers. They did not speak to each other about their recent ordeal. Each kept his thoughts to himself. They were left, too, to their own devices. Neither O'Riain nor his men had any time to spend with them during the day. When the men left the cabin they did not invite the boys to join them.

Their strength soon recovered. In contrast to Shane's gruel and the meagre rations of the McMahons the Cragg food was fit for a prince. In the space of a few days the hungry looks disappeared from their faces. But with the return of their health and strength came a longing for excitement. Happy as life was, they began to grow restless.

"Have you nothing at all to be doing," O'Riain's mother shouted at them one afternoon when she saw the four of them, staring at nothing in particular, sitting together around a doleful-looking Bran Óg.

The dog looked up expectantly but the four boys sheepishly shrugged their shoulders and said nothing.

"Well, then, make some use of yourselves," she said, "and catch a few rabbits maybe. Tell Eamon I said it."

When they told O'Riain he pointed to a low hill rising above the landscape about two miles to the west. "That's Gooig, the Hill above the Bog. It's alive with rabbits over there," he said, directing them to some snares at the back of the cabin.

"Take care you don't stray from Gooig," O'Riain's mother cautioned them from the door. "God alone knows the kind of people are wandering the hills these times."

They nodded in unison.

"Take care now," she warned. "Remember, Eamon has been able to rescue you once but he might not be able to do it again. If it was a patrol of Ironsides you ran into instead of a pair of miserable slave-hunters and sheep-stealers it would be a different story. None of these men is able to go hunting all over the place for you, risking their own lives."

Bran Óg jumped around with excitement as he sensed they were embarking on an adventure at last, and they, too, were giddy as they made their way towards Gooig. Just as Eamon had said, the hill was alive with rabbits, but as soon as the lads appeared with Bran Óg the furry creatures disappeared into their burrows.

"We should have left that beast at home," Brian said as they observed the deserted landscape.

Undaunted, Turlough and David took half of the snares, while Risteard and Brian took the remainder. With Bran Óg leaping from one to the other they set the snares around the hillside.

Turlough remembered setting snares in Coonagh with his father. He set a few near burrows where the grass looked a little trampled. Soon they were finished and looked at each other with smiles on their faces.

"Well, they won't come out and jump into them with us here," David said.

"Nor with him here," Brian said sourly, giving a dirty look at the unsuspecting Bran Óg, who thumped his tail against the ground as he waited for more entertainment.

"We'd best get away from here," Turlough said, "or the rabbits will stay underground all day."

"Can they hear us?" Risteard asked.

The others looked at him in bewilderment. Then Brian said, "They heard us when we were talking about them below at the house."

Risteard's eyebrows shot up until they seemed to disappear into his hair, and his eyes widened.

"They knew we were coming," David informed him.

"They did!" Risteard gasped.

"Rabbits can hear what's happening miles away," Brian said.

"They understand us then?" Risteard said.

"Some of them understand English as well," said David.

Risteard looked in wonder at the openings in the ground which housed the bilingual rabbits. "Well," he whispered, "we'd best leave them for a while." He moved away, lifting each leg off the ground as though walking through a field of eggs. His three companions and dog fell into step behind him.

"What will we do now?" David asked when Risteard deemed that they were far enough away from the rabbits' burrows.

"We'll see if we can find a few frogs or liebeens in the bog-holes down there."

"But go easy," Turlough cautioned, winking at David and Brian.

They put their fingers to their lips and signalled Risteard that there was to be silence. He looked at them, eyes wide open.

"The only chance we have is that the frogs up here only understand Latin," Brian whispered to him.

"And a little Greek," David added.

"And a little Greek," Brian agreed.

Risteard shook his head in disbelief.

"Yes," Turlough said. "The frogs of this place are known for their education. Every fool knows that."

As soon as they left the high ground the going underfoot became softer and wetter. Soon their progress was slowed as they had to pick their way carefully from clump to clump of solid ground. The sure-footed Bran Óg found it no trouble but soon the solid ground had all but disappeared and the boys had to watch their every step. All around them banks of turf waited for the turf-cutters of the coming summer. The bottoms of the banks were filled with brackish bog-water teeming with life – waterboatmen, newts, mature frogs and lively pinkeens.

They whooped with delight, Bran Óg barking with excitement, as they made their way from hole to hole. Though the frogs and pinkeens were plentiful, catching them was another problem. Try as they might all their efforts ended in failure.

Suddenly there was a splash and a cry of terror.

A bank overhanging a pool of dark water had given way under David. As Turlough stood on the bank laughing at his friend's predicament the ground beneath him caved in, too, and in a second he was beside the luckless David, up to his neck in bogwater. The fleet-footed Bran Óg jumped back and gave a belated warning bark. Despite their discomfort they were half-laughing at the sorry figure each cut in the other's eyes as they tried to get out, but found that there was nothing to grasp to secure them onto dry land.

"Come on, lads, help us out," Turlough appealed. "It's wet in here."

"I'm sure it is," Brian laughed. "Get yourselves out."

Bran Óg looked on, his head turned to one side as Turlough and David set to extricating themselves. They made no progress but became more and more angry as they failed to reach the bank. The more they struggled for a grip the more the bank broke away in their hands. The pair on dry land continued to laugh and joke.

Looking around helplessly, Turlough felt frozen. He saw David's face pinched tight with cold. An uncontrollable fit of shaking overcame his limbs. The two on land had stopped laughing.

"You'll have to pull us out," David called out through chattering teeth.

"With what?" Brian shouted, looking around. "There's nothing here. Unless we throw the dog in to you."

Turlough shook his fist at him and Brian backed away in mock-horror.

"Make a line out of your clothes," David shouted in desperation.

"You must be joking," Brian hooted.

"Brian, you'll have to help us. I can't stick this much longer," David shouted hoarsely.

Bran Óg barked at Brian and Risteard. Reluctantly they stripped off their jerkins and breeches and tied them lengthwise to make a rope for their stranded companions. With much huffing and puffing Turlough and David were brought onto dry land, panting and shivering. They were encased in smelly, mud-encrusted clothes but the other two, standing almost naked, were little better for in the rescue their clothes had become twisted and muddied beyond recognition. Trembling, they looked at each other in dismay.

"What will the old woman say?" Turlough looked at his clothes. "She warned us to stay out of harm."

"She'll probably skin us," Brian said, his arms wrapped around his chest. Sighing, he unknotted the garments. He unravelled them and threw Risteard's over to him. "Get them on fast before you die of cold," he ordered the small boy.

"A peace offering might help," Turlough suggested, as he tried to remove the brackish scum from his legs.

"Like what?" Brian snapped in disgust.

"Rabbit."

They managed a smile in spite of their condition and made their way back to the snares. They had struck lucky. There were five plump rabbits snared.

"This will keep her happy," Brian hollered as they set off home, well satisfied with their outing. Bran Óg barked loudly in agreement.

As the days passed the boys finally came to spend more time with O'Riain. He brought them to Castleconnell where they watched him expertly fish the pools for trout. Although none of this was new to Turlough, the other lads were fascinated by O'Riain's skill, and when they saw that Turlough was on equal terms with their hero they held him in high esteem. Then, one day as they fished the river, O'Riain informed them that a meeting was to be held that night. They joined him later in the cabin.

O'Riain looked seriously around the group.

"These lads will need to know the lie of the land too," he said, pointing to the four boys. "Some of our men have come back from Castleconnell," he spoke to them. "The people there are living in terror. They say the Ironsides are all over the place again."

His mother blessed herself. His men looked grim.

"I'll make a long story short," he continued. "Cromwell has passed a decree ordering anyone even remotely involved in the '41 rising to give up their land and go 'to Hell or to Connaught'."

"Where will it all end?" his mother said, turning away from them. "'Tis just one misfortune after the other." She shook her head in despair.

"Hell or Connaught," one of the men said, cursing.

"That's where I have to go, Connaught," Turlough spoke up.

"Then we'll have to look after you quickly," O'Riain said. "Garykennedy's your start, isn't it?"

"We'll lose the land," O'Riain's mother interrupted.

"We'll see about that," O'Riain said. He looked at his companions and they nodded. "There's plenty of mountains and woods for shelter yet, and whoever gets his hands on this piece of land will pay dearly for it."

"More killing," his mother said. "Is that to be it? More killing from this out. What else have we had these ten years past?"

"That's the way of it," O'Riain answered glumly.

"That boy there," the old woman raised her voice, looking at Risteard. "He's known nothing but fighting and killing all his life. He's never known a time or a day of peace."

O'Riain caught Turlough by the shoulder. "We're doing what

we can for them. We'll get this one to Garykennedy and let him start his long journey from there. At least," O'Riain gave Turlough a wry smile, "he'll be going the way that Cromwell wants."

His mother shook her head. "These lads should not be put on the road."

"They can stay as long as they want. I know that. But it's best to take the bull by the horns. This lad wants to travel."

Turlough could feel his excitement return.

"So get you off to sleep now and I'll have you up at cock's crow," O'Riain directed.

Turlough left the gathering. He had just collected his possessions for the journey ahead when the other boys returned. They faced each other silently across the room. Then David spoke. "We wish you good luck," he said simply.

It was still dark outside when O'Riain shook him awake. A breakfast had been prepared and he wasted no time eating it. As O'Riain made his way to the door Turlough looked across at his friends, still asleep in the straw. O'Riain turned. "Come," he ordered. "We have no time." Within minutes Turlough was mounted behind O'Riain with Bran Óg at the horse's heels.

Every mile of the road was made fascinating by O'Riain's knowledge and lore of the area. "This is the spot famous for birds' song. Nowhere else can you hear such singing. That's why it's called the Hill of the Sweet Throated Birds," he said of a place not far from Cragg. Each field and hill had a story to be told and O'Riain knew every cabin that they passed. But Turlough noticed, too, that many of the cabins were empty.

"There's many a good man gone from this place now," O'Riain admitted. "Ruined by war or driven out by Ironsides. The only thing increasing in this place is the wolf. Cromwell's government has a price of five pounds on the head of a priest and as much for the head of a wolf."

"Are there many?"

"The wolves are on the rise and the government wants them destroyed. Keep that in mind when you're on the road on your own. Wolves are the boys that would make short work of a traveller. Even one as young as yourself – you'd make a good supper for a wolf if he was hungry enough."

Turlough laughed. "Bran Óg will mind the two of us."

"Maybe. But be on your guard. Remember the two wolves you fell in with before. Bran Óg didn't save you then."

Turlough felt a chill. He had forgotten Murty and Shane. Somehow they seemed to belong to a dream – or nightmare.

They travelled in silence for a long time.

"Up ahead is a dangerous place," O'Riain spoke again. "It's the final place for crossing the Shannon before Limerick."

"What's dangerous about it?"

"Troops," O'Riain said sharply. "They're a law unto themselves. If they saw this fine horse under us, that would be the end of it."

They made their way along the shores of a lake. Gradually the ground began to rise and they climbed steadily among trees for mile after mile. Suddenly, Turlough gasped. Before them stretched the most beautiful scene he had ever witnessed.

"There's Lough Derg for you," O'Riain informed him.

The lake, shimmering in the early morning sun, was dotted with large and small islands. Away in the distance he could see a round tower on an island.

"What's that?"

"Holy Island, they call it around here. Inis Cealtra. Hundreds of years ago there was a monastery on it but the Vikings plundered it. Did you ever hear tell of the Vikings?"

Turlough nodded. His mother and father had often told him stories of how Brian Boru had died fighting them at the battle of Clontarf hundreds of years before.

"Maybe your friend in Garykennedy will take you out there. Whatever you do, don't go out on your own. It might look calm and peaceful now, but let the wind blow and it can be as dangerous as the mighty oceans."

There was little more speech between them. Turlough was hungry by afternoon but he didn't want to draw attention to it. The further they travelled, the more tense O'Riain seemed to become.

And then he stopped. He put his arm around Turlough and helped him to the ground, and then dismounted himself. He took a pouch from the horse and handed it to Turlough. It contained oaten cake.

"Are you sure you want to go on this journey?" he asked.

Turlough nodded, stuffing his mouth with a lump of the cake. O'Riain handed him another pouch, filled with water. Turlough took a greedy draught from it. Wiping the liquid from his lips he looked towards the lake. In truth, he was not as sure now as he had been when he set out that morning. He had a feeling that if he examined himself closely he would find that he was frightened of this journey, but something inside him fought to keep going. This was a journey he had to make. But to do it he would have to fight against loneliness as he parted from O'Riain and the comfort he took from his presence.

"Are you sure?" O'Riain asked again.

Turlough didn't want to speak. He nodded his head.

"Fine, boy. Straight ahead is Garykennedy, maybe a mile or so down this road. Let us be on our way."

O'Riain remounted and then put down his hand. Turlough caught it and with a swing was hoisted on behind him. O'Riain clicked the horse into motion.

XII

AT FIRST no one noticed the horse with its two riders. A party of women worked busily washing clothes in the waters of the lake. Some of them washed while others were flailing the wet clothes off flagstones by the shore. They chattered as they worked. Small children dashed to and fro among them.

A little girl was the first to see the strangers. She stopped playing and moved away from her companions. She shaded her eyes. Her sudden cry of alarm attracted the attention of the women. They stopped their labours and dashed onto the shore. From a distance Turlough and O'Riain could hear their cries. O'Riain reined the horse to a halt. They could see the women sheltering the children, all the while watching the mounted strangers.

"Come on, boy," O'Riain said softly. "Just walk in easy, we don't want to frighten them. Any stranger on a horse is bad news here." He dismounted and helped Turlough down. He gave the reins to Turlough who urged the horse slowly forward. Bran Óg walked by his side.

By the time they reached the cluster of huts a group of men had gathered on a piece of high ground, staring impassively at them. Bran Óg darted forward towards another dog and they eyed each other with suspicion. The children silently moved towards him.

The men made no sound. Their expressions were unchanging as O'Riain came forward, ahead of Turlough and the horse.

"God save you," O'Riain addressed the crowd.

There were murmurs of response.

"I'm looking for a boatman. McNamara is his name."

There was movement from the back of the group. A path opened. The roundest man Turlough had ever seen appeared out of the crowd. Short in height, he was as bald as an egg. A succession of chins seemed to descend to the top of his chest.

"Who wants him?" he asked. His voice sounded as if it came from inside an empty barrel. He held his arms loosely out from his sides as though he were about to engage in a wrestling match.

"The boy," O'Riain said, nodding his head back at Turlough.

"Who is he?"

"Tell him, boy."

"Turlough O'Brien."

The small fat man walked towards them, his shoulders rolling in a peculiar fashion. He stared hard at Turlough who was slightly taller than him.

"Why are you here?"

"My father ..."

"Who's your father?"

Turlough could find no words to speak. He fought the dryness in his throat but no words would come. He searched inside his jerkin for his pouch, and took out the silver circle his father had given him. He held it out.

The man took it and held it up to the light. His lips moved slightly but he did not say anything. He handed the token back to Turlough.

"He gave it to you?"

Turlough nodded.

"Where is he now?"

Turlough shook his head.

The man looked away from Turlough and stroked the horse's head. Then he looked at him again, as if he was trying to remember something he had long forgotten. He shook his head slowly and patted Turlough on the cheek.

"I'm McNamara," he said. "Come with me."

They made their way to a cabin amongst the cluster of huts

that looked out over the lake. Inside the cabin sat an old man and woman. After a few moments a woman as thin as McNamara was fat entered and whispered in his ear. He turned to Turlough.

"I know who you are and I'm glad to see you though sorry that it's without your father, may God be good to him. Now tell me, how did ye get here?"

Before O'Riain could say anything Turlough burst out with the whole story of what had happened since his family had left Coonagh for Limerick. McNamara, his back against a wall, listened, taking in every word. While Turlough spoke the fat man's face showed no expression; his eyes were as unblinking as an owl's.

"Brave lad," McNamara said when he had finished. "And you're a good friend," he nodded to O'Riain.

He signalled to the woman. She left the cabin and returned almost instantly with two jars. She filled small measures of whiskey for McNamara and O'Riain, and handed Turlough a crock of buttermilk.

"Can you help him?" O'Riain asked after a while.

"We'll do what we can to get him on his road when the time is right."

Turlough had a piece of bread thrust into his hand by the thin woman. He nibbled at it as the two spoke quietly. Finally O'Riain slapped Turlough on the shoulder.

"I must be on my way, boy. I still have a journey to make. Not as big as yours but I'd like to have the daylight with me these times."

Turlough accompanied him to his horse.

"You're among friends now," O'Riain said. "You'll make your journey to the Bay of Islands. Be wary on your way."

He mounted the horse, waved, and made his way at a trot through the playing children. Turlough watched until the horseman was out of sight.

The old man and woman were McNamara's father and mother and the thin woman was not his wife, as Turlough had thought, but his sister whose four children also shared the cabin. Her husband has been killed at Killaloe before Ireton's siege of Limerick.

"Your own wife?" Turlough enquired.

McNamara's huge body shook with laughter. "My own wife? Lord have mercy, I have no wife, lad." His sister looked on, smiling. "The lake is my wife. The boat might be my wife, too, I suppose, if a man could have two wives. But devil the wife I'd take of the human kind. Sure haven't I enough trouble on my hands without that." He chuckled to himself as he left the cabin.

The old couple had little to say. They sat in a corner, it seemed, all the time, shivering from some form of fever they had contracted. They whispered to each other and paid little heed to anything else that went on around them.

McNamara's oldest nephew, Con, was the same age as Turlough. He was a red-haired boy with blue eyes and a freckled face. He lived to fish and went on the lake with his uncle every time he could. All he was waiting for now, he confided to Turlough the first evening he arrived, was for the fly to be up. Turlough smiled. He had already heard Con ask McNamara when the fly would be up at least half a dozen times.

"Any day now, lad." McNamara had answered, clapping his hands together. "And you'll be the first to spot it, eh?"

Con nodded.

"Do you know about the fly?" McNamara asked Turlough.

"Sure how could he?" Con said impatiently.

Turlough suppressed a grin and said nothing. McNamara winked at him and patted Con on the head.

"A fisherman's son that doesn't know about the Mayfly?"

McNamara's belly rolled with his laughter. "Well, maybe they know nothing around the Shannon at Coonagh, eh? Look out closely at that lake tomorrow, lad, and you'll be looking at one of the best spots in Ireland for the Mayfly. Lough Derg. Mind you, I've heard tell of great things beyond the hills over in Galway. They talk about a place called Corrib, and I even heard of a great one in Mayo. But Lough Derg is the one, I tell you. She'll be up any day now. Then we'll have the fishing."

McNamara chuckled to himself in anticipation and looked over at his father, who was grinning toothlessly by the fire. "He remembers it, too," he said. "You do, don't you?" he roared over to the corner. The old man continued to grin. "Ah, God be with the youth of us," McNamara muttered to himself.

XIII

"How did your father die?" McNamara asked.

"He died in the fighting, I was told."

"Many's the good man died there on the walls of Limerick. We hear Hugh Dubh got away again, though. He cheated Cromwell at Clonmel and he cheated Ireton at Limerick. But look what happened to Ireton after he took Limerick. Died within days, we hear, and died roaring. The likes of them couldn't have luck with the misfortune they're bringing down on innocent people. They had to give up putting Hugh Dubh on trial, you know, and let him off to foreign parts. But luck wasn't with your father this time. And he was a lucky man, in his day." McNamara shaded his eyes and looked up, grinning. "Did he ever tell you of the fish we caught together, the two of us?"

Turlough had heard the story from his uncle, but he did not say so.

McNamara's voice shook with excitement. "He must have told you. My God, what a fish! A pike it was. Just the two of us out there, over towards the island beyond, for a whole day – or maybe it was two days."

"Two days."

"Aye. Maybe it was two. What matter. One day or two we spent out there, fighting with that fish. A pike. No fish like it, let alone a pike, was ever seen on that lake. It was the talk of the country around here when we brought it in. It took the two of us. You see the size of me? Well, I wasn't this wide then but I was wide, I was strong; and your father, he was a big man too. And it took the two of us to land the brute out of the water – the fiercest fight with a fish I was ever in. It was as heavy as a barrel full of drink. When we had it in, your father said: 'I hope we never get another one like that or it'll kill us both'."

"Did you eat it?"

"We did not," McNamara said, roaring with laughter. "But I must have you out to fish before you go off on your travels again."

"When the Mayfly comes up?"

The fat man's body rolled with laughter. "When the Mayfly is up – any day now. Look. See there." He caught Turlough's arm and pointed. Along the shore small figures moved slowly, their heads bent forward as they examined the waters of the lake intently. "The searchers are out and our Con at the head of them."

They watched the shore for a while. Then, speaking softly, McNamara broke the silence: "Is your mind set on your journey?"

"I have to do it," Turlough said.

The fat man sighed. "That's a frightful long journey for a lad of your age with nothing but a dog for company."

The two of them looked at Bran Óg stretched on the ground.

"You can stay here as long as you wish," McNamara said. "You'll know yourself when you want to leave. Aye. Just like the Mayfly. Who can say how it knows the time to come up, but it always does, give or take a few days." He smacked his lips loudly, as if he was already tasting the fish they would have.

"I was never on the lake for it," Turlough said, "but Uncle Seán and my father talked about it often enough."

McNamara thought for a moment. "I've seen it since I was that high and it's still as exciting as it ever was. The way it is, you see the odd one here and there for a day or so. Then suddenly the 'hatch' is up. They come up to the surface of the lake. It's a long thin thing, you wouldn't know what to make of it. For all the world you'd think it has a leather skin. It stays like that on top for a little while. Then the skin splits and out comes this buck with wings. It dries its wings first and then the poor devil has to reach the shore, and if it can make it it'll have to hide behind the rocks - like over there where the children are searching. You see?"

Turlough smiled at the fat man's excitement.

"You have to move fast, though. See the birds over there? When they know the eggs are hatched they'll come swarming out, flying in for the kill. So we'll have to pluck the Mayfly for our fishing before the gulls take them first. If they survive, they'll fly into the bushes over there. More of them than you can count. Then they head up into the air like that" - his hand moved up in an arc - "and they come down with a class of a twisting dance." He dug Turlough gently into the ribs. "And do you know what happens next? Well, I'll tell you: it dies."

Turlough gasped.

"He comes down out of his dance and falls down dying on the grass there. And the female that he danced with - she's a black, tattered thing - she fights her way out to the top of the water. Dying too. And dying, she lays her eggs."

Turlough, his mouth open in amazement, stared at him.

"Could you beat that? They have a dance of death to bring on the next generation. She lays her eggs and dies." He shook his head slowly, in wonder at this strange freak of nature.

The next morning it happened.

"They're up!"

By the time Turlough went outside McNamara was already directing the young ones into the bushes. The Mayfly is hard to recognise because it blends into its surroundings. "Be careful," he roared, joining the other men as they oversaw the delicate operation of taking up the fly. It had to be captured with the greatest delicacy, by the wings. Then it was placed inside a wooden case which was full of tiny holes.

They left Bran Óg tied by the side of the cabin. McNamara

rowed the boat, his long rod and line nestling under Turlough's feet, into the head of a shallow.

"It's cold," Turlough said.

"That's to the good," McNamara returned cheerfully. "We need the bit of a breeze for this, to carry the line out for us. We have to keep the fly on the top of the water, and the trick is to stop it being drowned in the waves. And if you can do that, then you'll have the good catch."

They began to drift downwind and Turlough watched eagerly as McNamara prepared to put a fly on to his hook. "Look at this here," he commanded.

Turlough leaned forward.

McNamara was holding a Mayfly delicately by the wings. "See this," he said. He held the fly under Turlough's nose.

Turlough examined it. Between the wings there was a sort of brown shield on the back. McNamara threaded a small hook through this shield and then placed another fly on the hook as well.

"Agh," McNamara grunted. "Now." Carefully he sent out his cast which was quickly taken by the breeze. The line filled out and the lure danced gently on top of the water. The fisherman watched it with great care, gently manipulating it against the little waves that threatened to drown it.

It proved to be one of the best openings of the Mayfly in memory. Every boat stayed out until late evening and every boat came back loaded with fish. Those on shore had known all day how it was proceeding from the signals that were being passed from boat to boat. They arrived back to a royal reception, and in every hut that night there was the smell of fish being cooked. That smell was still there when they rose next morning to resume the fishing, which continued for days.

By the end of the week Turlough was sick of eating fish.

The excitement caused by the Mayfly was barely over when

word arrived that there was a priest in the neighbourhood. There was to be a Mass, but McNamara would not say where it would be held.

"When the time comes, you'll find out," he answered Turlough's question.

"Why is it such a secret?"

McNamara frowned. "If the information gets into the wrong hands the priest's head will fall. One idle word can destroy a priest these times. Five pounds is a great deal of money to some."

A few mornings later he was shaken awake by McNamara. "Mass in Dromineer," he said. "Get yourself ready." The house was in an unusual state of excitement for such an early hour; all were ready to go except the old couple. Bran Óg was allowed to come, too.

The first silver streaks of dawn were appearing on the horizon when the small flotilla from Garykennedy reached the shoreland of Dromineer. Turlough looked in wonder at the large crowd which covered the field. The Mass was a hurried affair, and the crowd dispersed as soon as it was over. There was no time except for the most cursory of greetings: the people melted away into the morning until there was no evidence of the occasion except for the trampled grass.

They pushed off for home. The boat seemed to glide through the water and many of the other boats were soon astern. They rounded Mountaineer Rock.

"What's that?" Turlough shouted, pointing to the shore.

McNamara twisted his head. "Infantry!"

With his hand above his eyes Turlough examined the shore. Suddenly his heart jumped. There was the unmistakable figure of Peadar, he was certain. He was dancing along the fringe of the troopers, pointing with his whip towards the boat. Further back, Turlough thought he saw Murty and Shane.

"We've been betrayed," yelled McNamara. "God's curse on whoever set them on us."

He strove to get the boat as far offshore as he could.

A trooper came forward to the edge of the shore. He knelt down and sighted his musket on them.

"Lord have mercy on us," McNamara's sister cried, trying to group her children around her. Turlough put his arms around one of the smaller children.

"Down, blast the lot of you," McNamara roared. "Get down as low as you can!"

They tried to hide in the bottom of the boat but there were too many of them. Peeping up, Turlough saw that the soldier was still kneeling with his sights on them. He felt as if his breathing had been stilled, waiting for the shot to fire out.

"No fear," McNamara called to them. "He'll not reach us."

They heard a faint bang and a puff of smoke.

"He'll have to do better than that," McNamara called out cheerily.

"They won't give up," Turlough said. Beside him, Bran Óg growled. "Don't you see? They followed me."

McNamara glared at him. "Who?" he barked.

"Them," Turlough called out. He pointed at the figures on the shore. "They're the ones I told you about. They're the ones that captured me."

"Bad luck to the whole crew," McNamara's sister said, holding her brood of children tightly.

"Do they recognise you?" McNamara called out.

"You see the one in front? I know him for sure."

McNamara pulled harder on the oars, putting distance between the boat and the shore. "It might not be you," he said when they had put the soldiers out of sight. "They're most likely slavers, all right, but they could be looking to catch a priest. A priest is worth more to them than a boy any day of the week."

Turlough didn't answer. The sight of Peadar had sent a chill of fear through him. And Peadar had seen him.

"Not far more now," he heard McNamara say. But hardly were the words spoken when Con cried out: "Look!"

They stared in the direction of his shaking hand. Behind their village, from another cluster of huts higher up on the hill, clouds of black smoke billowed into the sky.

"They've fired Portroe," McNamara gasped. He stopped rowing. His head slumped down on his chest. It was some time before he spoke, and when he did his voice was heavy as lead.

"You're finished here now." He caught Turlough by the arm. "Those hunters won't give up on you – you know too much about them. If they can, they'll hunt you down. I can feel it in my bones."

Turlough hesitated. If the McNamaras were in trouble he wanted to be with them.

"You've no business staying here," McNamara said. "We'll manage our own affairs; you have to look after yours. This is the time for you to leave." His voice was hard.

Turlough nodded.

"Good. We'll make for the far shore and you'll make your way by land following the water to Portumna." He changed the course of the boat.

"See there," McNamara called to him, pointing to an island. "That's Hare Island. One time not too long ago, a couple of hares were being chased by a few hounds and their only hope of escape was over the thin ice and on to that island. The dogs were too heavy for the ice. But when the hares felt it safe to return to the shore the ice had melted. So there they are to this day, safe but imprisoned."

As they rounded the island McNamara called out again. "Remember now, Turlough, be careful. Especially be careful of people on their own. Give your trust very slowly. Mind out for the people who ask too many questions. Don't let anyone know you're alone. When you leave a place, do it quietly and secretly. And be careful where and when you light fires."

"Where do I go from Portumna?"

"Head by the bridge. There's a big red-headed man by the name of Tom O'Halloran – tell him I sent you and he'll guide you across the right way if there's any danger."

They reached the shore.

"Off with you, boy, and God guide you. Take these with you." From underneath his seat he took some hooks and a line. "Put these with your things. They might of use to you yet."

Bran Óg jumped ashore and Turlough followed him. McNamara and the others waved. The boat moved away.

Turlough turned his back to his friends and glided into the woods which stretched down to the shoreline. Bran Óg, his tail up, plodded quietly beside him.

XIV

FOR A while Turlough and Bran Óg could hear the voices of McNamara and his boat-load as they made their way back home across the lake. Soon the voices were gone and the only sounds were the panting of Bran Óg and the singing of the birds.

He sat down for a moment to take his bearings. As always, he had his pouch with him. Wrapped around his waist, it felt so familiar he no longer even noticed it. There was a great reassurance in knowing it held the flint that Tomás had given him, and now the hooks and line of McNamara. Tomás's gift had earned its passage: the days in Cragg had taught him to be an expert fire lighter when there was rabbit to roast in the company of his friends in the hunt.

They walked for hours. A rumbling in his stomach reminded him that he was without food. He looked to the water, trying to shrug off the pangs of hunger. Follow the lake, McNamara had said. Turlough repeated the words to himself as he continued close to the trees, keeping the waters of the lake clearly in view.

The day grew hot. Even though the trees provided shade he soon felt uncomfortable. Bran Óg trotted from time to the time to the edge of the waters to slake his thirst and occasionally Turlough followed his lead, grateful for the cool water as it slid down his throat. He splashed some onto his face and moved on.

His hunger grew worse. He stopped and looked around. Although he did not want to encounter people, he half-wished that he might. Then suddenly Bran Óg darted away as if he had heard something. Turlough tried to follow the direction in which Bran Óg was heading but soon lost track.

He waited for an age. Once he called out "Bran Óg!" The

shout came out a hollow croak. His voice, affected by the heat and hunger, sounded rusty and cracked. He had a pain in his head. He sat by the water's edge, watching the shadows of the clouds drifting by in the waters. He fought against worrying. There was crackling from the trees. Turlough's heart skipped. Then, in a mad careering dash, his ears flopping up and down, Bran Óg burst out of the undergrowth.

Turlough stared in disbelief at his dog. He looked a sight, his mouth full of feathers! Had he meant to catch them a bird to eat? Turlough pulled some feather's from Bran Óg's moist mouth and examined them. They were black as pitch. Bran Óg looked up at him, then hung his head and sat back, sniffing at the captive feathers as though he somehow expected them to turn into something edible.

"Ah, Bran Óg," Turlough shook his head. "You're no dog for the wild, are you?" He stood up. "No rest now, boy," he tapped Bran Óg on the head. "We still have miles to make."

They headed off, keeping close to the water's edge, but soon the land rose into hills and brought them out into the sun. From the height Turlough could see back to where, only a short time ago, the lake had been covered with fishermen. It was empty now. The waters of the lake were a shimmering mirror of shifting greens and blues and whites. Small islands dotted the lake. On the Tipperary side the hills rose, blue and green in their seasonal finery. And still smoke from the burning of Portroe curled into the sky.

Turlough had lost all idea of how long they had been travelling, but he could see that the light of the day was fading. The pain in his stomach was now a constant, nagging cramp. So was the pain in his feet, swollen in his wretched brogues. He sat down with his back against a tree. Bran Óg joined him, panting expectantly, full of energy.

A small creek nearby drained into the lake, its water swishing down the incline. Turlough listened to the rhythm of the water, and then his ear was caught by something else. His eyes lit up: the creek was alive with frogs. In no time he had one clutched between his hands. Deftly he transfixed it with a hook and made his way to the lake shore. With a small twig as a float he tossed line and bait out on the water. Eagerly he kept his eyes on the twig. For a while there was no movement, but then the float bobbled, disappeared. Turlough whooped with joy and began to haul the line.

Soon he had a fire blazing and his hunger pains were forgotten as the succulent fish gave him sustenance. Darkness had fallen by the time he finished eating. Comfortable in the warmth of the fire, his belly full, he prepared himself for sleep.

At the first streak of light they resumed their journey. They walked until Turlough judged that it was about noon. By then they had climbed a considerable distance and the sun was again becoming oppressive. His arms were red from the sun and, as he looked down at his torn brogues, Turlough realised that his feet would not take this daily punishment.

He commanded a view of the lake on all sides. Shortly he would be leaving the lower part of the lake behind. He looked ahead and, with a start, realised that right across from him a column of dark smoke was unfurling itself lazily into the cloudless sky. Another village put to the fire!

They continued walking. Absently, he plodded onward and rounded the hill. Below was woodland. And smoke! Cautiously now, Turlough made his way forward. Where there was smoke there must be people – and food. But as he came nearer he realised that it was not chimney-smoke but a burned-out cabin. He looked around slowly, seeking movement. Nothing stirred. It must have been a fisherman's place, he thought. What had happened? Was it possible that the soldiers had crossed the lake and were now burning out habitations on this side as they had on the other? But why would they burn out one lone cabin? There was no sign of any bodies.

There was nothing to be learned here. Calling Bran Óg, he started off again, ignoring the pains in his feet.

The next cabin they encountered was intact. Hidden in a hollow, it seemed deserted. Turlough eyed it from the shelter of some ash trees. A cake of bread rested on a ledge by the side of the dwelling. He took a few slow steps forward.

A low growl sounded from the house. Startled, Turlough moved back, edging his way to the shelter of the trees.

A man appeared in the doorway with a wolfhound. He carried a sharpened stick and held it at the ready as if he expected to be attacked. But he saw no one. The man was not completely satisfied. Beckoning his dog and grasping the stick firmly, he moved cautiously out from the protection of the cabin, searching the surrounds with his eyes. From within a woman's voice called out. The man turned, gave one last look around, and went back inside.

Turlough's instincts told him that he should retreat. But hunger was a greater spur than fear. He must get food.

Holding his breath, he crept out from the grove, signalling Bran Óg to remain. Now he could see the warm soda cake. The fresh smell from the cake travelled across, tantalising him. He moved forward. He could no longer see the front of the house, the man or the dog. Voices came from the cabin. He took another step forward. A piece of stick snapped under his foot. He froze. Nothing happened. The murmuring continued within the cabin. He took another step, fighting the impulse to dash forward and seize the cake, now almost within his grasp. He reached out.

"Thief!"

He was knocked sideways by a cuff to the side of the head and before he could regain his balance he was held by the neck. He fought in vain to release himself.

Bran Óg dashed from the trees but before he could reach Turlough he was cut off by the arrival of the wolfhound, the hairs on its neck bristling. Its low deep growl made Turlough's blood turn cold.

"Hold," the man said and the wolfhound stood guard, keeping the barking Bran Óg at bay.

Turlough was turned round as the man changed his grip and caught him by the shoulder.

He was a large man. Long black hair and a beard obscured most of his face. His dark eyes stared into Turlough's.

"Now, boy, what's this you're doing?"

Turlough held out the cake.

"Hungry, eh?"

Turlough nodded.

"We're all hungry these times, boy. You're not the only one who needs to fill his belly."

"What is it?" a woman's voice called out from the cabin.

The man turned round to answer, and relaxed his grip for an instant. Turlough pulled away, holding on to the cake. He heard his shirt ripping. The man lunged at him but Turlough ducked and tripped him. The man put his hands out to save himself from falling to the ground. Turlough ran. Even as he did so from the corner of his eye he saw the wolfhound, watching its master, make an uncertain movement.

Turlough and Bran Óg raced for the trees. He could hear the man's roar from behind.

"Come back, boy, come back."

Panting for breath, Turlough ran until he felt his chest would burst. Completely out of breath and heaving as if he could never again be able to breathe quietly, he hunkered down by a tree and examined his cake. Gasping, he gave thanks for the providence that had saved him from another day of hunger.

He started. He was not out of danger yet. In the distance he could hear the baying of the wolfhound. They were being followed!

The water! He called Bran Óg and raced for the lake. Hugging the edge of the lake, they waded forward. The waters were cooling on his legs and feet. He tore off the edges of the cake as they continued, passing pieces of it to Bran Óg. Now and again, his mouth full of the dry bread, he stooped down and greedily scooped up handfuls of water. At last his panic subsided, and they stopped.

By evening they had put many more miles behind them, and that night, as they rested beside the lake, Turlough felt a stirring of contentment. With Bran Óg to warm him, he looked at the sky until the stars became blurred and he fell asleep, his hands across the front of his shirt, cradling the remains of the cake, his food for the next day's travelling.

He was drenched when he awoke. The night's rain had soaked through his clothes. The precious cake was wet. Turlough examined it disconsolately, realising that it was either eat it or eat nothing. He and Bran Óg breakfasted on the remains of the bread and resumed their journey along the lake side.

To his surprise Turlough found that it was easier to walk in the rain than in sunshine. The rain did not let up for the whole day and darkness came earlier that night. They walked on in the darkness.

Then, in the distance, he saw a twinkle that wasn't a star. He stopped and watched for it to move, but it didn't move. They headed towards the light. There was more than one: they must be lanterns. Turlough held his breath. Could it be a camp? That would mean soldiers. He stopped. Or could it be a village?

XV

THE BRIDGE was visible through the darkness. As Turlough came closer he saw that there was a cabin beside the bridge.
He knocked gently on the door.
"Who's there?" a gruff voice called out.
He knocked again.
"Who's there? I'll not answer until I know who's there!"
"Turlough O'Brien."
"Who?"
"O'Brien."
"What O'Brien?"
"Turlough O'Brien."
"I don't know any Turlough O'Brien."
"From McNamara in Garykennedy."

A shutter was pulled on the other side of the door. It opened suddenly and a hand reached out and grabbed Turlough by the arm, pulling him in so forcefully and shutting the door behind him so quickly that Bran Óg was left behind.

He blinked in the darkness. The only light was from a small candle held by an old woman in a shawl. She was crouched in the corner of the room, surrounded by three young children. All of them looked at him in silence.

The man came round to the front of Turlough. He was of medium height. Even in the gloom of the cabin his red hair stood out. He had a short red beard and eyes of piercing blue. His broad shoulders and muscled arms indicated a man of powerful strength.

"Are you Mister O'Halloran?"
The man licked his lips uneasily.
"Maybe," he said at last.
"The boatman in Garykennedy – he said you would aid me."

The whines of Bran Óg outside the door distracted them. The man opened the door to let Bran Óg enter, then banged it shut and refastened the wooden shutter.

"How can I aid you?"

"I'm making my way to Mayo."

"Mayo, God help us," O'Halloran said. "What would anyone want to go there for?"

"I have people there."

"A drop of milk, Máirín," O'Halloran said over his shoulder. One of the children filled a ladle with milk and he gestured to Turlough to take it. "Drink it slowly, lad," he said, stooping down beside Turlough. "Did you travel from Garykennedy yourself?"

Turlough nodded.

"And how is McNamara?"

"He was grand when I saw him. But anything might have happened since. I think I saw the place on fire."

"Lord look down on us, the times is in it," O'Halloran was shocked. "The country is crawling with English and Lord knows how many places they've put to the fire and how many they've put to the sword."

Turlough finished drinking the milk.

"You've a long road behind you and a longer one ahead of you. You'd best rest, and leave your story for the morning."

Turlough lay back on a bed of straw and Bran Óg snuggled down beside him. He took off his brogues and felt his swollen feet. Though they throbbed with pain, within minutes he was asleep.

When he woke up the cabin was already astir. There was no sign of O'Halloran but the old woman and the three children, a boy and two girls, were finishing a meal of stirabout. A little girl, her thin body and spindly legs showing through her ragged clothes, came over and handed him some stirabout in a chipped bowl. He had to stop himself from snatching it from her. He muttered a hasty thanks and started to wolf down the food. The little girl jumped back from him.

"Did you sleep well, little boy?" the old woman asked. Her face was sunken and she had no teeth. Her voice was a cracked rasp.

"I did," he said, and then added, "and my thanks to you and yours for the bed."

The old woman said nothing but gave a dry little laugh.

O'Halloran, on his return, sat down on a *súgán* chair. He ate a piece of cheese and soda cake without speaking. Then he took a pipe from his pocket and slowly began to fill it. This operation was observed in silence by the rest of the household. When he had it filled he passed it to the old woman. She chuckled to herself as she sucked on it. While she smoked she looked away from the rest of them as though they might be a distraction to her pleasure. Turlough thought that she looked as if she was in a dream. Every now and then she made chuckling little noises to herself, and her eyes had a vacant look. Now O'Halloran filled another pipe, which he shared with his small son. The little boy took a short shallow draw on the pipe, standing by his father's knee, and then moved over to the open doorway and blew the smoke out.

"Would you chance a pull yourself?" O'Halloran offered Turlough.

Turlough declined.

"Now," O'Halloran settled himself back into his chair, "tell me what you've been doing with yourself."

Turlough began his story. All the while he was speaking O'Halloran watched him closely; the piercing blue eyes hardly ever left Turlough's face. He found this uncomfortable, as though his honesty was being examined. The children also listened, their pinched faces gazing at Turlough. And every so often the old lady, though she never seemed to take her attention away from her pipe, made a clucking, sympathetic noise as Turlough continued with his tale.

"You've had a hard time of it," O'Halloran observed. "The small man you describe is the worst of all."

"Do you know him?"

"I don't know him. And I don't want to know him. But I have heard of him. He's Peadar O'Rourke. He's an uncle to the other two. There's no devilment known to God or man but they'll get up to it. They hunt everything from boys to wolves to priests. You wouldn't want to fall into their hands again."

"Are they known here?"

"They're known here and in many other places as well. They come from Roscommon, I hear. They linked up with the English and tagged along with them for this time past. Making themselves useful to the English for a few shillings. They're a bad crew. There's no shortage of them in Ireland now since this last lot of Englishmen came in. They're not men at all. They prey on the young and the old and the unfortunate."

O'Halloran stopped speaking, his head on his chest, as if he were thinking deeply. Moments passed before he looked up again. "You'd be wise to travel on your way, I think, as soon as we can get you fixed up." O'Halloran's pipe had gone out. He sucked on it absently. "Take care you heed what I say. The road I'm sending you on is the only real road for where you want to go. But it's a dangerous route, for it is infested by wolves."

"Wolves?"

"This country's ridden with wolves now. The English pay a big bounty on every one caught, and there are men around at this minute making a living off the wolves. You'd best be very careful."

"I'll light fires."

"Will you?" O'Halloran laughed. The old woman, still sucking on her empty pipe, gave a cackle. "Well, indeed and you might. But think of this. What keeps the wolves away is only a signal to another kind of wolf. The kind like the small man from Roscommon and his nephews. They're looking for the likes of you, out on your own, and the fire is the signal for them."

O'Halloran looked down at Turlough's feet and sighed. "We'll have to find you a better pair of brogues than those. You'll not get far if you're not better shod." He called out something to the old woman and she shuffled out of the cabin, still puffing on her pipe.

"Is your mother very old?" Turlough asked.

O'Halloran stared at him. "My mother?"

"Herself." Turlough nodded at the door through which the old woman had just gone out.

O'Halloran's face darkened. "That's not my mother, lad. That's my wife."

Turlough could feel his face redden with embarrassment.

"Sure how could you know?" O'Halloran said, clapping him on the shoulder. "We've had some savage times in these parts and it's affected her – the same as the rest of us." He stared at the floor until one of the children suddenly caught his arm and pointed to the door.

A shadow fell across the door. "God save all here," a voice called from outside.

A tall, thin young man entered. He was so tall that he had to bend almost double to enter the cabin, and when he was inside he continued to stoop to keep his head from banging into the thatch. He had an old piece of sacking across his arm.

"Is this the *gasúr?*" he asked. His voice was thin and reedy, too, and because of his height seemed to fall down out of the thatch. "God save you, young fellow," he said, holding out his long thin hand.

Turlough's hand disappeared into the giant maw of the stranger's. As the other man took his hand away Turlough saw fingers so long they reminded him of eels. He almost expected to see them squirm as their owner restored them to his side.

"Turlough, this is my cousin Art," O'Halloran said, looking up at the giant and smiling.

Art threw the piece of sacking to the ground. "Let him try these," he said as a pair of cowhide shoes tumbled to the floor.

"The lad that had them will want them no more," O'Halloran said quietly.

"Let them go in a good cause then," Art said.

Turlough looked at his new brogues, delighted at the comfort they would mean for his blistered feet. He stumbled out his thanks.

"Where's the lad heading for?" Art asked.

"Mayo," O'Halloran said.

"Well then, he'd best make his road for Galway first."

"Aye," O'Halloran agreed. "He'll be lost if he doesn't. If he was to head straight from here – just to follow the setting sun – he'd be sure to make it, and then strike north for Mayo." O'Halloran absently fiddled with his pipe. "He'll have to do the best he can."

"And take no heed of strangers," Art cautioned Turlough once more. "Best not to look for guidance when you leave this place."

O'Halloran nodded agreement.

"Do you hear all I'm saying?" Art asked suddenly.

"I do," Turlough answered.

"It'll maybe cost you your life if you don't. You did well to make it this far, but the hardest part is ahead of you. You have no friends to fall back on from here out. You're on your own."

XVI

O'HALLORAN SHOOK him awake early the next morning. He had a crock full of steaming oatmeal ready. "'Tis a cold morning," he growled, rubbing his hands together. Turlough could feel the cold pierce through his skimpy clothes.

"We've this for you, too," O'Halloran pointed to a parcel of food on the table. "If you don't eat too much at one time, there will be enough for a few days. And there's some scraps for himself as well," he added, nodding at Bran Óg.

Turlough started to speak but O'Halloran cut him short. "There's no time to waste," he said. "Go on, now, lad, straight over the bridge and be on your way." He almost pushed Turlough and Bran Óg out the door.

Outside, a light mist was falling. The sky was a sleety grey and showed no break in the clouds. Turlough's new footwear gave him great comfort and he felt confident in his strength as he moved away from the slumbering town, out into the countryside. The light drizzle of the early morning slowly faded, but the day remained cold.

Turlough stopped only very briefly to eat a little of O'Halloran's provisions and feed a few scraps to Bran Óg. O'Halloran had packed the wallet with soda cake and pieces of salted pork. The saltiness of the pork made Turlough thirsty. For the first time he became conscious that he had moved away from the lake. He had lived with the ceaseless lapping of its waters for so long that he had taken its companionship for granted.

He passed the time by telling himself stories and, when he tired of those, he recited rhymes from his childhood. As the day continued he chatted half to Bran Óg, half to himself, remarking on the features of the countryside they were passing through. He had seen so many new places since Coonagh! He stopped to sit on a rock and nibble one more piece of pork, and then he determined to keep going until dark.

By dusk Turlough was once more in the vicinity of woodland. It was not the same as the woodland further south. This was silent, deep and dark, as if it were the guardian of a secret. He stood on a knoll and looked down on the wood. His legs, he realised, were trembling slightly. He did not feel safe on the outside of the wood, yet he feared to enter.

This is silly, Turlough told himself, deciding that he would find a place to sleep just inside the first line of trees so that he would be able to look out. Still he felt uneasy. He watched Bran Óg to see if he had any signal to offer, but Bran Óg marched beside him as though they were heading for a warm cabin.

He lay back against a tree on the edge of the wood. Bran Óg snuggled down beside him and after a few minutes the warmth of the dog eased Turlough into slumber.

Suddenly he woke up.

He looked around, rubbing sleep from his eyes. Something had moved. Bran Óg lay quietly beside him. Then the dog stirred and stretched. Turlough watched, but Bran Óg showed no anxiety.

The sound that suddenly pierced the wood was deep. It was so fierce it made Turlough tremble; then it slowly died away. Turlough cowered closer to the tree, cold sweat breaking out on his body. He jumped when it came again. But this time it was high-pitched, from a different source. Turlough's spine tingled: it was a human scream. Coldness spread through his body like a drenching of icy water. He pulled himself upwards, grasping hold of Bran Óg. The deep baying came again. Now it was nearer and he knew what it was.

Wolves!

He looked out. It was impossible to see anything in the dark.

There was nowhere to run. Stuffing the soda cake inside his shirt, he swung himself upwards onto the nearest branch and clambered into the lower reaches of the tree. He leaned down and caught Bran Óg by the scruff of the neck. He took a deep breath and then, summoning all his strength, snatched Bran Óg off the ground. The dog began to yelp. Turlough hit him sharply on the nose and held him tightly, but Bran Óg would not keep still. He had to wrestle with the dog to hold him fast, and nearly lost his foothold in the tree. He whispered urgently to Bran Óg in an attempt to soothe him; he tightened his grip, but Bran Óg would not be held in check. Before Turlough could control him, he jumped out of his arms and landed on the grass, rolled over, and ran off into the trees.

Turlough looked after him in dismay. There was nothing he could do to bring the dog back now. He began to climb higher for more safety. From his perch he looked into the darkness; he stood and strained to hear. There was a rustling of something approaching through the brushwood. Bran Óg returning.

There was a loud burst in the undergrowth and two wolves broke through at the same instant. They stopped underneath the tree and circled it, sniffing. One wolf looked up, its bright malevolent eyes shining like two tongues of fire. Its mouth broke into a snarl.

Turlough crouched lower and looked in horror at the snarling beasts. He tightened his grip on the branch level with his chest and looked down. They returned his stare with unbending gaze.

He lost track of time. The two beasts prowled around the tree, waiting. Now and again Turlough had to stand up to take the stiffness from his joints. He was afraid that if he became too stiff he would fall from his perch. He threw down some soda cake in the hope that it might appease the wild creatures. One wolf sniffed at it and turned his head away.

They waited.

A thousand times he must have looked at the sky to see if there was any sign of light. He had a faint hope that the light of day would drive the wolves away. But still they waited.

At first when he heard voices Turlough thought that he was imagining things. He listened again but there was no sound except for a slight sighing through the branches of the trees.

Then it came again, the sound of voices. It was still dark, although dawn could not be far away: a faint streak of light could be seen on the edge of the sky.

Turlough looked down. They had heard it too. The two wolves stirred uneasily, growled to each other and looked into the wood in the direction of the voices. Turlough thought he heard the sound of a dog barking.

Bran Óg! Had he brought rescue?

He saw lights moving. With mounting excitement he was sure he could smell the burning sticks. From his height Turlough marked the progress of his rescuers in the glow of torches which flickered on and off through the trees. The wolves turned towards the sounds and the lights growing nearer, and growled at them. But these were not the full-throated growls of earlier; now they were uncertain. They made short restless movements, pawing round the base of the tree. Almost before Turlough realised it, they had disappeared into the wood.

He stood up unsteadily, the branch creaking beneath him, and slowly stretched his legs. He eased his body down through the branches until he was on the lowest one, then he swung himself off and fell onto the ground.

He lay there, recovering his breath, as the lights in the wood came closer. He could get the acrid scent of burning pitch. They came out of the trees, the lights held in front of the faces of the torch-bearers. Bran Óg ran from among the oncomers and launched himself at his master, licking his face. Turlough caught him and moved him to one side as the torch-bearers came closer. He heard the snuffling of horses. Many horses. Behind the torch-bearers was a dark shadow on horseback.

He stood up.

Turlough cried out as the whip curled around his legs and brought him to the ground, jarring his body. His head thumped off the earth, sending stars showering before his eyes.

A shape bent over him in the gloom. He looked up, conscious only of the stinging in his legs where the whip had wrapped itself around his skin.

Under the flickering flame, a pair of dark eyes in a pale face looked into his. "Well, my young friend. Well met, eh?" hissed Peadar.

Turlough looked around in bewilderment. Two shadowy figures leaned forward. With a groan Turlough realised who they were.

XVII

Turlough's hands were tied behind his back and he was thrown to the ground. Bran Óg was by his feet. His captors quickly made a brushwood fire and settled down around it to wait for the morning light.

"Only for your dog there we might have missed you," Shane sneered at him. He clapped Murty on the back and the two of them bent double with laughter.

"How did you get here?" Peadar asked softly, his whip dangling over his arm.

Bran Óg growled. Turlough held him firmly around the neck.

"Well, boy, I'm asking again: how did you get here?"

"I made my way here," Turlough said.

"On your own!" Shane shouted out.

"I don't believe you made it on your own, boy," Peadar said.

"Someone helped you," said Murty.

Turlough said nothing.

"I wonder who?" Murty mused to himself.

"O'Riain," Peadar spat the name out.

Shane laughed grimly. "That's who it was. And if I ever lay eyes on him again, I'll dig his grave for him and welcome."

"He's meddled once too often in our affairs," Peadar said to his two nephews.

"The soldiers have taken care of him," Shane laughed again. They took care of your friends in Garykennedy, too," he added for Turlough's benefit.

"They've all moved to new quarters," Peadar said. "Ah, yes, and O'Riain and his crowd, too, are shifted off their place in the hills to make way for planters and their betters."

"And if O'Riain ever falls among us ..." Shane began again, but Peadar cut him off.

"This won't get us far. We'll bide our time till the day comes. In the meantime, we'll take the road for Ballinasloe."

They took some food from their saddle-bags and chewed on it, ignoring their captive. Although Peadar seemed impatient, none of them was anxious to leave their fire for the cold morning air.

"'Tis a pity the priests aren't more plentiful," Murty was saying. "They pay far better than boys and they're not as hard to capture as wolves."

"True for you," Shane agreed. "Make it up and you'll see: 'twould take nearly forty boys to equal one priesteen. And they'd need to be sturdy ones at that."

"Five pounds the *sagart*," Murty chortled. "And that one was hunted up and down the land, from Offaly down to Kerry and back through Limerick and Tipperary, and devil the one could lay a hand on him. They were smiling when they handed over every one of those coins."

"Oh," Shane crooned with delight. "Wouldn't you pray for a few more like that? We'd be set up for the rest of our lives."

"Set for life, is it," Peadar looked at the two of them. "You'd best hush." He glanced over at Turlough.

"What ails you?" Murty asked sharply.

"If every man or woman in Munster or even here in Connaught hears that we made our money on the head of that priest, each one of us is done for. We're finished. Now, I don't mind one way or the other how I go, but I'd sooner not bring it down on myself by talking about it. There's probably a bog-hole at the end of the road for each one of us if not something worse, but I'd sooner not jump into mine yet, if none of you mind."

The cold rasp of his voice cast a chill that was even colder than the coming dawn. His two nephews looked away from him. Their eyes avoided Turlough also. "Yerra, who's to know," Murty said eventually, "except him. And he's in no position to tell tales on anyone."

"Hasn't he a tongue in his head?" Peadar asked.

Turlough looked over. Murty had taken a knife from his belt – the knife that Tomás had given Turlough. Turlough sighed. Tomás and Coonagh seemed such a long time past now. Murty came over, kicked Bran Óg from Turlough's heels, and knelt on the ground beside him. He pointed the knife straight at Turlough's mouth.

"He has a tongue now, all right," he said.

"Whisht," Shane snapped. "We're in no danger."

"Not now," Peadar whispered.

"But later?" Murty asked softly.

"Mark my words," Peadar said to the two of them, "those guineas could be the dearest that ever were minted. No matter if you cut out his heart and his tongue."

Murty drew the knife back from Turlough's face and returned it to his belt.

A few hours later they prepared to move on. The horses were readied for the journey to the horse fair in Ballinasloe. There were eight in number. They were sorry-looking beasts, rough-skinned and slow-moving. They moved with their heads towards the ground. The best that could be said for them, Turlough thought, was that they were a form of transport and better than enduring a forced march on foot.

Murty hauled him to his feet.

"Tie his hands to the front," Peadar instructed his nephew.

"No. He'll ... "

"With his hands tied behind his back he'll spend most of his time falling off the horse. He'll only hold us up."

Murty did as he was bid. He caught Turlough's hands and crossed them at the wrists, lashing them tightly together with the rope. He produced a longer length of rope and tied it around Turlough's waist.

He pointed to the feeblest of the animals. "Get up on this one," he grunted, heaving Turlough onto the beast. Turlough took the reins into his tethered hands, conscious that the wretched animal might collapse under his weight.

Soon they were on their way, Bran Óg trailing behind them at a safe distance. Judging their course by the sun, which had begun to climb into the early morning sky, Turlough could see that they were heading north, more or less following the course of the Shannon for the moment.

Progress was slow but relentless. There was little talk among his captors, and an eerie silence clothed the land. It was as if the country lay under a pall of fear. Even the wildlife was strangely quiet but for the flight of a solitary heron or the plaintive cry of the snipe. They travelled for hours in silence before Murty signalled a halt.

"We'd best give these garrans a rest," he shouted to his companions.

"True for you," Shane said. "They look to be dying on their feet."

They dismounted. Murty signalled Turlough to throw his leg across the side of the horse. He caught him and helped him down.

"Don't stand near those horses," he ordered. "Stand where I can see you."

As the horses ravenously attacked such grass as was available on the stony ground, Turlough's captors were settling down to rest when, with one accord, the entire group froze as a high-pitched howl rent the silence. Then deep throaty growls carried on the crisp air. Wild and primordial, they were sounds to make the blood run cold.

"Wolves," Shane said.

"God's curse on the plague of them." His voice was shaky. "Would they be the same ones from last night?"

Nobody answered him.

"The horses!" Peadar shouted.

Murty and Shane dashed forward at the same time and caught the reins of the horses. They looped the reins across the branch of a nearby tree.

Peadar put his hand to his ear and slowly turned himself around as he tried to fix the direction of the cry. Although some moments had passed it was as if they could still feel the intense urgency of that wild cry in the air.

"We'll move on," Peadar said. He signalled the others to mount up.

Murty watched sourly as Turlough mounted. "Take care you don't manage to get yourself separated from the rest of us, brat."

"Is this your time to run again, boy?" Shane asked.

"No. It is not," Turlough retorted sullenly.

Peadar looked at him with a wintry smile. "No? Remember it. Any wolf will have the heart out of the horse in seconds and then it'll be your throat. Remember that."

Turlough knew that he was right. There would be no protection from a wolf if it caught him in the open.

They rounded the corner of a small hill. The howling came again. This time it was different. It was as if it had been multiplied.

"There," Shane shouted, pointing.

They turned to look. A white movement startled them as it broke into view and then disappeared, followed by a black streak travelling at breakneck speed.

"We're safe now," Murty sat back on his horse. "The sheep will keep them satisfied this day anyway."

In another few paces they could look down on the slaughter. A pack of wolves had cornered a small flock of sheep in a hollow of the glen. One by one they were torn down by their savage attackers. Turlough felt his stomach heave in protest at the spectacle. The bleats of the sheep filled the air, their high-pitched cries of fear mixing with the ferocious growls of their killers.

Turlough looked at the others, engrossed in the scene below them. The wolves tore the sheep into pieces of raw meat, a devil's feast as wolves ran crazily from one carcass to another, gorging themselves with mouthfuls of the bloody flesh. Murty watched the scene, his throat working convulsively as the wolves went about their grizzly meal, his mouth moving as though he were an animal himself.

Turlough worked his tethered hands cautiously to the knot on the rope around his waist. His fingers were so numb he had difficulty in feeling the knot. He forced his mind to concentrate on getting feeling back into his hands and fingers. Flexing his fingers put pressure on the rope, chafing his wrists even more, but he persisted, fighting the pain. He manoeuvred one hand into position over the knot at his waist; he could feel its shape.

He continued to work at it, all the while watching Murty. He risked a quick look down: it was still intact. He manipulated the rope again and felt the knot loosen. He let it be.

He heard his captors speaking to each other and looked up; the wolves had ended their attack and were beginning to scatter, leaving the remains of their grisly feast behind.

"We'd best move on from this," Peadar said.

They turned their mounts away from the bloody scene.

"How safe is it?" Shane asked.

"'Tisn't," Peadar said shortly. "They're hungry. We'll need eyes in the back of our heads from this out."

"They'll not attack us," Shane said.

"Won't they? If that's what you think, you'd best be ready to learn different. If they're hungry enough they'll attack anything that moves."

As they rode along Murty recounted details of what they had

seen, asking the others if they had noticed. His voice rang with excitement. His companions threw back short replies, but he ignored their lack of interest, talking as if they had not seen what he had. With his reins he held the rope attached to Turlough, who followed a few paces behind. Holding his breath as if Murty might hear it, Turlough moved his hands to the knot once more. With one quick flick he knew that the knot would come undone.

He examined his situation. He had a bad saddle but it would stay in place. What of his horse? It was probably not much worse than those ridden by his companions. But the only time before this he had ridden a horse had been with Uncle Seán, and that had ended in a fall.

He drew in his breath. He would count to ten. It was now or never. Before he started counting he placed his hands across the knot. He tugged. Yes, it would come. He held the end piece tightly between his fingers and he began to count. One.

Murty continued to talk excitedly to his companions. Two. Turlough stared straight ahead. Three. Peadar shouted something at Murty. Four. Shane cursed. Five.

Murty looked back at Turlough. Turlough froze. Murty smiled to himself and turned forward again. Six. Seven. Turlough placed his feet out from his horse's sides. Eight. He pulled on the knot. Nine. He caught the reins in clenched hands and ten! dug his feet into the horse's flanks.

The horse gave a hoarse whinny. Turlough felt his heart stop. Would it not move? With a jerk it broke into a gallop. His captors looked on in disbelief as the horse and rider sped by them.

Turlough guided his mount off the trail, along the line of least resistance, skirting the edge of a rising field with a copse in the distance. His captors' yells and curses were soon behind him. He moved on to the rising ground, heading for the copse.

Ignoring the pain in his tethered wrists, he clutched the reins for dear life. If he could reach the trees and make for the other side of them before any of his pursuers reached the rise he might be able to fool them.

He didn't dare look back. His horse may have been taken by surprise but for all his broken condition he had the wind for the run. So did Bran Óg, catching up alongside with his ears streaming in the wind. Turlough, refreshed by the wind rushing past his face and exhilarated by the pace of his horse, gave a yelp of triumph as they approached the copse. He circled it and took his bearings.

Bare ground sloped down on the far side of the glen, and offered no cover. He stared down, his horse champing and snorting. In the open he knew that he had no hope. Bran Óg barked urgently.

There was nothing for it. Turlough dug into the horse's flanks and guided him onto the falling ground. They descended at speed and dashed across the field making for the horizon. He looked behind: no pursuers were visible. Turlough urged the horse on. Out of the corner of his eye he saw movement in the distance. He had been looking in the wrong direction for his pursuers! He was being attacked from two sides in a pincer movement.

Pushing the horse as fast as it would move, he decided to make a break and see if he could outride them by going forward. "Go on, boy," he urged.

Bran Óg gave a yelp. Turlough looked around. His faithful dog was flagging. And so, he realised, was his horse.

His pursuers were closing in, cutting off his forward path.

He clenched the reins tightly and pulled. His mount responded, veering away from the oncoming rider, but his pace slowed as he turned.

The rider whipped his horse and dashed after Turlough.

Turlough could make out his face. It was Murty, riding hard, his face distorted with rage. He rode at full pelt as Turlough's horse slowed from exhaustion.

Turlough pulled up. He drew his leg across and slid down from the horse. Bran Óg, panting, fell at his feet.

Murty was off his horse before it had even stopped. He came running forward. Turlough braced himself against the onrush of the big man. A blow on the face sent him spinning along the ground. His tied hands were under him when he fell and pain shot through his shoulder as it took the force of the fall. Dazed, he felt nothing for a moment and was turned over on his back. He blinked in the sunlight as the shadow of Murty's fist hit him again across the face.

He heard a voice shouting. It was his own. There was another voice but he could not identify it. He saw the glint of a blade. He lay transfixed as it came forward. He twisted away but was held. He called out but no sound came. He winced with pain and tasted blood dribbling into his mouth. Murty's hoarse voice roared obscenities at him. Turlough kicked out and Murty fell backward, clutching his thigh. He kicked out again and Murty moved back, still holding the knife, then regained his balance and came forward. His voice twisted in anger and hate. Turlough braced himself to sit up, his eyes fixed on the knife.

Murty screamed as the knife was flicked out of his hand by Peadar's whip. "No more!" he shouted at Murty and pulled Turlough upright. "We have money to make out of him!" He tore a strip off Turlough's shirt. "You're scarred, boy. Be grateful that's all that's happened to you."

Turlough held the cloth to his face as they placed him back on his shivering horse.

XVIII

PEADAR TIED the rope around his waist this time and pulled Turlough's horse beside him. Grim-faced, his hand plucking at his beard, Murty watched Turlough's every move. Turlough's cheek throbbed from the knife wound and his shoulder was stiff and sore.

"I like the wrestling at the fair," Shane tried to strike up some conversation with the others. "Ballinasloe is great for wrestling."

"Why don't you do some of it if you like it that much," Murty gave back.

"And the anvil-throwing. You were good at that once, Uncle," Shane shouted at Peadar. Peadar made no answer.

When they reached the outskirts of Ballinasloe Peadar signalled them to stop. Heated whispered discussion took place between the three of them. While Turlough could not make out what was said, he could see that frequent glances were thrown his way.

Peadar walked back to him. "Listen carefully," he said. "Let there be no mistake about this. One false move out of you and it's the last you'll ever make. You've had your chance. You'll not be worth the trouble of keeping if you try again. Do you understand me?"

Turlough nodded.

"And you two, keep a tight grip on those beasts or all our time is wasted. Do you mind me?"

"We hear you," Murty shouted.

"Right so. We'll go and sell our horses and see what God brings us in the way of luck."

They started down the hill, Murty and Shane keeping tight reins on the unmounted animals. Bran Óg trotted alongside Turlough's mount; dirty now and bedraggled, he was in bad shape. As they reached the flat, Turlough caught his breath. Never in his wildest dreams had he imagined that there were so many horses in the world. He drank in the sight. This was a gathering greater than any he had ever seen in Limerick, even before the war started. Every colour and shape and size of horse seemed to be present across the acres of trampled fields along the banks of the river Suck.

Slowly they made their way into the sea of horse-flesh and men, women, children, vagabonds, horse-tanglers and mountebanks. Turlough's eyes opened wider still as he took in the acrobats and musicians, and the fire-eaters devouring flame in front of throngs of astonished youngsters. He saw also the unwelcome figures of Roundheads but this did not seem to bother any of his companions.

Turlough was pushed ahead of his captors, but in the end even they found a spectacle which stopped them in their tracks.

"Here, look here," Shane shouted out, as excited as a small boy. "The strong men are at it!"

Turlough looked up eagerly. Two giants, or so they seemed to him, were about to try each other's strength in an anvil-throwing contest.

"The smithies," Murty said, drawing in his breath.

One smith was short with a chest like a barrel. His head was completely without hair but his face, of a red and freckled hue, was covered by a thick red beard. Around his waist was a wide leather belt with a buckle the size of a fist. His opponent was taller but thin and muscular. By contrast he had a full head of black hair but his face, although dark in colour, had no beard. He wore a leather apron.

The dark smith was the first to throw. Eyes bulging, he lifted the lump of iron, and with a gasp threw it forward. Turlough held his breath – as did all those around him – as the anvil shot forward. The anvil thudded onto the ground and the spectators released their breaths at the same time; one great gasping sound, almost a groan, rose into the air. It was a mighty throw. The man himself eyed it with interest and then shook his head. He did not think much of it. But the spectators did not share his doubts. They nodded in appreciation of such an awesome demonstration of strength.

Now they looked to the other contestant. The red-haired smith rubbed his hands vigorously against each other and then ran them against his huge thighs. His back was to Turlough who could see the cord-like muscles rippling in the blocky man's back. His nostrils shivered like those of a horse. He drew in a huge lungful of air and his chest inflated until it seemed it must burst. He took his stance, legs braced for the lift. He lifted the anvil without effort. Silence fell on the crowd as he raised the weight above his shoulders. With an explosive effort, drawing a gasp from deep within himself, he hurled the anvil forward a good two feet beyond that of his rival. Now, raising his hand in the air in jubilation, he called out "Beat that!"

The dark smith took up the challenge. He lifted the anvil. His movements were slow, as though he had all the time in the world. He took what seemed to be a short run and then unleashed a fling which shot the anvil several inches beyond the red-haired smithy's throw. A great cheer went up from his supporters. The betting men were counting their winnings.

But the red-haired one was not ready to surrender. He went forward and, taking several deep breaths, he lifted the anvil. The veins stood out in his neck. Beads of sweat stood poised on his bald head. With a scream of triumph or pain he launched the anvil into the air with such raw, brutal strength that the crowd were silenced. The markers looked and then looked again. A length of *súgán* rope was produced; the distances were measured and re-measured. Astonishment circulated among the spectators. The contestants had drawn to a dead heat.

Now the respective camps went into a huddle. It was finally decided that one throw more would decide the contest.

They pulled straws to decide the order of the final throw. This time the red-beard was to go first. He unbuckled his belt and, pulling it as tight as it would go, he buckled it again. Very slowly, with painful deliberation, he picked up the anvil. He sucked in air as though to save his life, his enormous chest bulging. He bent his knees and with a roar that seemed to disappear into the sky he launched his anvil half a foot beyond the marker stick. A wild roar rose from his followers.

"There's no one in the four corners of Ireland will match that," someone said.

"Troth and we will see. There's another man here to go yet, don't forget," came an indignant cry from the rival camp.

The calls went back and forth between the two groups. All the while, the black-haired smith waited. Turlough watched him closely. The man's eyes were fixed on the horizon as he waited without interest for the banter to die down. His throat worked as if he was chewing something. His jaw was clenched in firm determination. As the noise abated, and he waited for complete stillness, he flexed his muscles.

The shouting stopped. All eyes were on him. He looked around as if only now had he become aware that he was the centre of attention. With careful deliberation he stripped off his leather apron. He raised the iron as high as he could and held it for a moment before hurling it into the air. It was the fastest throw of the competition.

The marchers rushed forward and the *súgán* was called for again.

All around him Turlough could sense the crowd holding in its breath. Then the hair on the back of his head rose as a shout, louder than all the other thunderous shouts that had punctuated the contest, rang out. He could not see what was happening as the crowd pressed forward. Beside him, Peadar, his small size stopping him, too, from seeing the result, jumped up and down, cursing with rage and excitement, but holding tightly onto Turlough's arm.

But now the dark smith was visible, raised high on the shoulders of his followers. He was the champion. When they let him down he embraced his defeated opponent. Around him the lucky gamblers collected their winnings while losers turned away.

"Come," Peadar directed Murty and Shane.

Holding the animals tightly, they jostled their way through the crowd. Women in shawls bustled around them with small children in tow, chattering away among themselves. A child smiled up at Turlough and he grinned back. He stumbled and felt a grip on the back of his neck as he collected his balance.

"Take care where you go, lad," a strange voice shouted at him.

"He's mine," Peadar shouted at the stranger.

Turlough turned back as the painful grip was released. The grip belonged to a big man with a ruddy face and a scar under his chin. Turlough looked at him blankly. He had seen the face before, somewhere.

"There's no one will take the brat from you," the man said, staring coldly at Turlough and turning away.

"Get on, you clumsy oaf," Peadar growled, giving Turlough a kick.

Gritting his teeth, Turlough made his way forward. The crush of the crowd and the pain in his ankle made him feel queasy. He stumbled again and again was kicked, this time by Murty. By now the ground was little more than slushy mud from the thousands of people trampling through the fields, and he found it harder and harder to maintain his balance when anyone pushed against him.

"Stop up," Murty ordered.

Turlough stopped and looked hesitantly behind him. They had reached the fringes of the crowd. Peadar and Shane had got into conversation with a wiry little man wearing a leather jerkin. He had grey hair and a red dent on his forehead, the rest of which was corrugated with creases. He began to examine the horses.

"You must be giving away these beasts," he said to Peadar. "Out of charity to the poor things, the way they won't die on your hands."

Murty snorted indignantly, all the while keeping a firm grip on Turlough's shoulder.

"You call yourself a tangler," Shane said. "Do you not know decent horse-flesh when you see it?"

"Horse-flesh!" the tangler exclaimed. "Flesh is right. Good for giving to dogs or maybe for feeding to pigs, that's all that flesh is worth, I say."

"I always heard the men of Galway were no judge of horses," Peadar answered. "I heard it from Donegal down to Cork."

"Then you didn't see many horses on your travels," the tangler shouted back, with a smile that showed crooked teeth, "if you think these hay-baskets add up to horse-flesh in these times."

"Take a good look at them," Shane said. "They've been on the road a while. That's all that's wrong with them. They're a bit tired. With a bit of rest they'll be in fine fettle."

The tangler smiled at him for a moment. "Mind you, with a bit of luck I might get a quartermaster to make an offer for some meat to feed to the Roundheads."

"Go on! They're good for years yet," Murty threw in indignantly.

"They're the sorriest-looking poor creatures I've seen since I came here. If I took them off your hands itself – and God knows it would be an almighty act of charity if I did – I don't know what I'd do with them."

"Go on so," Peadar urged, "make your best offer."

The tangler shook his head. "No. I'm sorry, gentlemen, but there's nothing I can do for that lot. Sure the bones are sticking out through them!"

"A bit of feeding is all they need," Murty said. "Look at them. A few feeds of oats and they'll be jumping up and raring to go."

"To go where?" the tangler asked in disbelief. "They won't make it to the knacker's yard from the look of them."

"You're a hard man," Shane said.

"A mighty hard man," Murty confirmed.

The tangler looked from one to the other. His expression changed from laughter to sadness as if sorry that he could not help out two such decent men. But he had no more to say for the moment. There was silence as they all looked at the objects of the bargaining.

"Hard, is it?" Peadar began again. "You're a stupid man that doesn't know healthy beasts when you see them. Tired but healthy is what they are."

"Hah," the tangler raised his voice in disgust. "Tired and dying is more like it!"

Turlough lost interest in the argument, and looked idly around for a while. As he turned back to the four men making the deal, he found that Peadar and his two nephews were gathered in earnest whispered argument. The tangler stood to one side. Turlough watched them closely. The tangler had managed a curious thing, he observed: he had the three men at each other's throats. Peadar was biting at his two nephews, and Murty and Shane were not happy with each other, either. Turlough looked at the tangler with a new curiosity. His face was turned away from the men, but he was watching them out of the corner of his eye. Then he noticed that Turlough was looking at him and he frowned. He turned away, but as he did so he winked at Turlough. Turlough made a slight movement with his hand; there was no reaction from the tangler. He was sure that he had not made a mistake, but the tangler's face was now set in stony indifference.

Murty stepped away from the others, his face black with anger. The tangler went over and put his arm around Murty's shoulders and whispered in his ear. Murty pushed the tangler's arm away and scowled even more bitterly. The tangler laughed.

"Right, men," he roared out. "I can't be here all day looking on at you three. I have money to make. So what will it be. Deal or no deal?"

They stopped quarrelling among themselves and started bargaining again. This was the last part of the ritual, it seemed, for very quickly they had agreed terms and a deal was struck. The tangler spat on his hand, offered it to Murty who spat on his own before accepting the tangler's.

"Now," the tangler said when he had paid out the money, "is the *gasúr* here for sale? He doesn't look as if he'd eat much and he'd make a handy drover along the roads with that old dog beside him, eh?"

Peadar shook his head.

Turlough held his breath.

"Well, is he too precious or what?" the tangler asked.

"He's not for sale," Peadar growled.

"I didn't think he was one of yourselves," the tangler said quietly.

"Well, he is, then," Murty said.

"That must be why you take such good care of him. The way you're holding on to him, he must be worth gold or silver." The tangler smiled when Murty cursed at him.

"Aye," Peadar said. "We're afraid he might get lost in the crowd."

"Or maybe be run over by a horse," the tangler said.

"Or maybe get a knife in the ribs," Shane said softly.

The tangler was about to say something. His mouth opened and then, with a foolish expression, he clamped it shut again. He nodded and, grasping the sets of reins, he led the horses away.

Chortling to themselves at having sold off their nags, the three took Turlough and Bran Óg and made their way back into the press of people. Now they stopped for a while to watch a horse-shoe-throwing contest; around them fire-eaters, tumblers and jugglers added a festive touch to the serious work of horse-trading.

Their business done, Murty and Shane were anxious for drink. Peadar watched with distrust as they sought out a drink-seller. When they found one they whooped with delight. They threw money to him, then held their heads back as they drank deeply, like men who had not drunk anything for days. Peadar, gripping Turlough with one arm and holding the reins of the four horses, looked on sourly. Turlough was thirsty himself but he was not offered anything to drink. Despite Peadar's curses Shane and Murty insisted on another drink before leaving the drink-seller, their faces covered in broad grins as they pushed onward.

As soon as they had Ballinasloe left behind they tied Turlough again. Now they made steady, uneventful progress. As dusk closed in on them Peadar called the group to a halt. The horses were tethered to a few trees beside a small lake and a fire was quickly lit. They cooked some food and Turlough ate his share greedily. Bran Óg, who had begun to keep a safe distance from Murty and the others, crept closer.

"Eat well, boy," Murty shouted. "We want you fine and strong for Galway."

Shane joined in the laughter and even Peadar permitted himself a wintry smile.

XIX

A KICK IN the ribs thrust him across the ground.

"Get up, boy."

The damp grass passed Turlough's face in a blur. When he stopped tumbling he was on his back. The pain in his shoulder and rib-cage throbbed. He blinked his eyes open. The trees overhead threatened to fall on him.

"Up, brat," Murty barked, untying the ropes.

He stood up. Bran Óg, warned by the man's voice, hung back.

Turlough looked around slowly. There was no sight of Peadar and Shane. He became frightened. He could feel along his legs the cold lashes of Peadar's whip. Where could the other two have disappeared to?

Murty turned away and looked towards the horses.

"Would you try one of those?" he barked at Turlough.

"No," Turlough answered.

"Liar!"

"No, I wouldn't."

"Then you're a coward."

Turlough felt as though his feet stood on thin ice.

"Which are you, boy: a liar or a coward? You're either one or the other."

"No."

"No? You're too innocent, is it?"

"No."

"Not innocent. If you're not innocent you must be guilty. Hah." He let out a shout of triumph. "What are you guilty of, boy? You've damned yourself. What is it you're guilty of?"

Murty rocked on his stubby feet, his hands on his hips as though to balance himself.

"I'm not a liar."

"Then you're a coward."

Turlough held his breath. Frightened, his eyes searched frantically for an escape. Should he run for it?

Murty squinted at him. "You bold-faced brat. I'd like to see you try," he hissed.

"Try what?"

"Make a break."

Turlough continued to stare. He felt that he was within minutes of being hurt or even killed. Murty hated him.

"You're alone, boy, completely alone – remember that. And there's no one to miss you one way or the other." Murty gloated in his power.

A voice called out a short distance away: Peadar and Shane were returning. Murty's eyes flicked in anger. He turned to Turlough. "I'll see to you yet," he threatened.

Peadar and Shane arrived, a pair of rabbits dangling from their fists. "Meat," Peadar announced. He gathered the animals together in one hand, grasping them by the necks, and sniffed. Then he threw them to the ground. "Now, let you get a fire together," he ordered Murty. He looked from Murty to Turlough. "What were you doing?"

"I was helping our young friend here to understand how to survive."

Peadar scowled. "He's looking rightly shook after his lesson, isn't he?"

"We live in hard times, I was telling him."

Peadar eyes his nephew coldly. "I don't want him damaged."

Murty's voice lost its cocky tone. "He has only himself to blame if he makes a break for it," he said sullenly.

"You never know," Shane butted in slyly. "Someone might be prepared to take him in. He might be handy enough to put out on a hill and mind a few sheep, like St Patrick.

"We'd best eat and get back on the road if we're to make Galway this side of Christmas," Shane continued. He began busily skinning the rabbits. As the others set about the fire, he skewered the little animals on a spit of wood. He placed the spit across the fire, resting it on two forked sticks, and watched it for a few moments to see that the spit was properly positioned.

It was some time before the rabbits were cooked. Again it was Shane who inspected the breakfast. When he was satisfied that the rabbits were done he searched around until he found a large wide flat rock which he placed under the spit. He pulled out the supports and the cooked rabbits fell onto the stone. He touched one of them tentatively and nodded in satisfaction.

Within minutes the meat was divided out between the four of them and they ate without pause. Turlough made a pile of bones to feed to Bran Og, who watched them from a short distance. Hungry as he was, the dog hung back.

"We'll get water on the way out," Peadar said. "We have to cross the river beyond." He nodded across the fields.

"Will it be any bother to cross?" Murty asked.

"You saw it yourself," Shane said scornfully. "We'll ford it without bother."

Shane stamped out the fire and they rode slowly away from the camp. The earth was warming up as the sun shone from a cloudless sky. They rode in single file, Shane and Murty ahead of Turlough, and Peadar bringing up the rear. Turlough looked from side to side but he did not look behind. He could feel the stare in his back.

The two leading riders halted. They were facing a river. Although it seemed to be moving sluggishly, it was clearly deep at the point where they had stopped.

"We'll go further down," Murty insisted.

"We'll maybe give a try here," Shane said.

"Maybe we'll not," Peadar came up to them. "It would want

to be easier to cross than this."

"For you it'd need to be no more than a hand high," Shane muttered. He urged his mount on.

They moved along the bank of the river. Bran Óg had run ahead of them, sniffing out this strange land. At a bend in the river where the water had slowed in a wide meandering loop, Peadar called them to a halt.

"I'll try it first," Shane said, urging his horse into the water.

They watched from the bank while he slowly guided the horse onwards. The beast was reluctant and shied back from the water, but Shane dug his heels in and pressed forward, clicking his teeth at the straining animal. "Easy, now, easy," Murty advised from the bank, as if he were the rider in charge of the horse.

Man and horse reached midstream. The water was up to the middle of Shane's boots. "I'd say that's the depth," he called back to them.

"I'm not going in," Peadar shouted.

"We'll make it," Murty said.

"We'll not," Peadar said loudly. "Me and the boy – we'll not make it."

"Of course you will," Shane roared.

But Peadar turned suddenly and rode back from the bank. "Come here, boy," he shouted at Turlough.

Murty cursed and rode his horse into the water. His horse, taking courage from the sight of its fellow in the middle of the stream, made no resistance. He joined Shane in midstream and they huddled together. From the safety of the river-bank Peadar leaned forward as if in hope of overhearing his nephews.

Bran Óg barked.

"Shut him up," Peadar said angrily.

Turlough looked back at Bran Óg. He was turned away from them, barking softly to himself. Turlough screwed up his eyes and his heart skipped a beat. In the distance he could see a bunch of horsemen approaching fast.

Murty and Shane moved through the water, heads down as they carefully guided the nervous horses across the river.

Then Peadar noticed the horsemen. His sharp intake of breath was like a hiss. He caught Turlough's arm and wheeled their horses round in retreat. But he was too late. Two of the horsemen had seen the move and broke away to cut them off. They held guns in front of them. As they bore down on Peadar and Turlough, Turlough recognised the rider in front. The tangler! He sped forward.

"One move, my friend," the tangler shouted a warning to Peadar, "and you are a dead little man."

With an oath Peadar pulled his horse to a halt.

"We didn't forget you, lad," the tangler said to Turlough. He nodded across the river to where the main group of riders stood in a hollow set back from the bank, in waiting for Shane and Murty.

"Why don't we shoot this priest-killer, Seán," the tangler said to his companion.

"We'll see what Eamon wants first. But give me an excuse ..." Seán tapped his gun.

Eamon. Eamon O'Riain! Turlough twisted his gaze to the other side of the river.

Only when Shane and Murty had emerged from the water and mounted the bank did they realise the trap. They swung round on their horses to call back to Peadar, and stopped in dismay when they saw that Peadar was captured. Shane shouted to Murty. Suddenly they split. Shane spurred his horse down the bank while Murty drove his furiously in the other direction.

As Turlough watched, O'Riain and his companion rose from their hiding place and rode in a diagonal line cutting off Murty's escape. His only retreat was through the river. He swung his horse on to the bank leading down to the water but the animal resisted, rearing its forelegs. Scrabbling to regain its footing on the loose bank, the horse began to fall. Murty jumped as it fell clumsily to the ground.

Murty's knife reflected the sun as he drew it from his belt. He held it up in front of him as O'Riain's horsemen ranged themselves around him. O'Riain dismounted.

"Gut him," Peadar hissed fiercely from the river-bank.

"He won't be the one gutted, my little friend," the tangler said.

O'Riain had no weapon. He slowly moved in towards Murty. Holding himself straight, knife in hand, the big man looked with contempt at O'Riain. Then he crouched, holding his long knife stiffly out from his stomach, moving sideways in an attempt to find an opening. When O'Riain was within reach Murty whipped the weapon in a dazzling arc: it seemed to Turlough that he could hear the blade cutting the air with a sharp whirr. O'Riain stepped back quickly. Murty overbalanced but recovered before O'Riain could gain an advantage.

Turlough held his breath as he watched the unarmed man facing the knife. Murty made a sudden lunge: O'Riain sidestepped. Beside him was a branch of wood; he ducked down to pick it up.

Murty was on him like a flash. Turlough could almost feel the weight of Murty's body as the big man heaved himself forward. The knife flashed towards O'Riain's chest. O'Riain rolled to one side and took the blow on the upper arm. A long crimson line appeared through his shirt.

O'Riain's left arm went limp, bathed in blood down to his hand, but the piece of wood he clasped in his right hand was as steady as if it were rooted to the ground. He drew it up to block off another vicious thrust from the knife; it lodged in the wood for an instant but Murty tugged it free. O'Riain swung the stick through the air, aiming at the big man's upper body. It caught his ribs, but caused no great damage. Murty drew himself up to his full height, knife still at the ready, then crouched forward. His lips were parted, his teeth clenched together in a mirthless grin.

O'Riain jabbed at him, but he failed to make contact. Murty's knife sliced through the air, directed at O'Riain's face. O'Riain pulled his head back just in time. Murty bent low, concentrating on finding a gap in O'Riain's guard. O'Riain's stick suddenly shot forward and jabbed him in the thigh. It struck heavily. Murty was knocked off balance for a moment.

That moment was enough. O'Riain darted in, parrying a thrust of the knife, and lodged his stick in the big man's midriff. Murty doubled up, still desperately holding on to his knife. He tried to straighten but another heavy blow landed across his shoulders. Gasping for breath, he howled out with pain. He flashed the knife through the air, keeping O'Riain back, as he struggled desperately to stay upright. His feet gave way under him; he fell onto the bank and rolled slowly towards the river. He lay there face-down.

O'Riain jabbed him in the back with his stick. There was no reaction. O'Riain stepped into the water. Catching the body by the jerkin, he pulled it towards him. A companion entered the water and together they dragged Murty onto the bank and turned him over. His eyes gazed sightlessly towards the sky. Water dropped from his beard. The knife protruded from his stomach.

"May your souls be damned!" Peadar screamed.

"May you learn to pray before you die," the tangler glared at him. "We'll cross the river now."

"I'll not cross," Peadar shouted.

"Do you want to rot here?" The tangler pointed the gun at Peadar's chest.

When they reached the other side one of O'Riain's men was

tending his injured arm. The knife-cut was not deep and they bandaged it with a strip of cloth torn from a shirt.

O'Riain looked up and smiled at Turlough. "We're getting tired taking you away from these wolves," he laughed.

"What will we do with this one?" the tangler asked.

"I know what I'd like to do," a voice said grimly. "And with the other one when we catch him."

"You'll never get him now," Peadar sneered at them all. Shane had made good his escape.

"He'll not get far," the tangler said. "The word is out what ye did to that poor priest at Garykennedy. Someone will stretch ye, sooner or later."

"Leave him. We'll not burden ourselves with him," O'Riain commanded. "Let him loose." He ignored the rumblings of discontent from his men. "Now listen," he said sharply. "We're not going to kill him in cold blood."

"Why not?" an angry voice called out. "They kill innocents!"

O'Riain looked around at his men. "Look at him," he said. "Where can he go? He's known. He'll be safe nowhere. Leave him to his fate."

"He could meet up with soldiers and give us away."

"He can go to his own place in Roscommon."

"Can he?" O'Riain looked at his followers. No one said anything. "I don't think he can. Do you know where he's making for?" he asked Turlough.

"I heard them say Galway."

"Yes: not Roscommon. The word is travelling before him; he can't go home. No one knows him in Galway, most likely, but they will. We don't need to do anything. No one will ever mistake that little limb of the devil for anyone else," O'Riain said. He walked slowly across to Peadar and yanked him to his feet.

"You'll give me my horses," Peadar said.

"No."

"That's robbery!"

O'Riain laughed. "You might say that. You should report us to your friends the soldiers."

"But I've miles ahead of me!"

"Then you'd best not waste any more time here," Turlough shouted out.

Peadar shrugged, turning to Turlough. "You were bad luck to us, boy. If 'twas Limerick again, I'd slit your throat as soon as look at you."

"You'd best leave while you still can," O'Riain said quietly.

Peadar pushed his way through the group.

"Take your friend," O'Riain said.

Peadar stopped and looked around, his face a picture of disbelief.

"How?" he shouted.

"Take him."

Peadar stopped for a moment, then stooped over Murty's body. He pulled it upright and struggled to get it over his shoulder, bracing his feet to secure balance. After a moment he started forward and began his journey away from the river, his nephew's body on his back.

O'Riain and men watched until the man and his burden had disappeared into the distance.

"He'll not get far carrying that," the tangler said.

O'Riain mounted his horse. "The devil mend him. Let him bury him when he's too tired to go any further," he said.

XX

BARKING LOUDLY, Bran Óg scampered ahead of the leading horse. As they rode through the Galway countryside O'Riain told Turlough they had been watching him the whole time at the Ballinasloe fair, and had assigned the tangler to keep track of his three captors. He had held his men back because if Turlough's captors had bolted it might not have been possible to catch up with them.

"I thought I knew one of the men I saw at the fair, all right. Where are the others?" Turlough asked as they rode westwards.

O'Riain pointed ahead. "A few miles up there. We left them resting. These are changed times," he continued grimly. "We've lost some men. We came across from Tipperary but we'll go back when the time is right. We'll fight for what's ours." He clenched his fist and waved it in the air. "We're not beaten," he shouted.

His men gave a cheer when they heard his voice.

"The last time I saw you you were on foot and now you have a fine horse," O'Riain looked at Turlough smiling.

"With the compliments of three of the finest villains you'll ever clap an eye on," the tangler shouted.

"What happened to the lads at Cragg?" Turlough asked.

"We found homes for them. But they're probably scattered now, too."

"How is Risteard?"

"That little devil. He's the finest. He's as healthy as a trout. He's found a home for himself, you might say. And you? You haven't found your home yet."

"It won't be long now," Turlough said. "I'll be there soon." But he knew he didn't feel as confident as he might sound.

"Indeed," O'Riain said doubtfully. "And how did you fall in

with those boyos back there again?"

Turlough told him the story. O'Riain said nothing until Turlough was finished.

"So you'll go on?" he asked after a while.

"I'll go on," Turlough said defiantly.

They said little until they reached the grove by the stream where the rest of the band was waiting for their leader.

"Turlough!"

He looked down from his horse at the boy below him and he hardly recognised him. Risteard! Looking plump with rosy cheeks and bright eyes. Turlough jumped down from his mount and was grabbed around the waist by the smaller boy who spun him round and round until he nearly threw him off balance. They laughed at each other, neither able to say anything.

"Well," O'Riain shouted, clapping each of them on the back, "I told you he'd found a home. We kept him!"

"And the others?" Turlough asked hopefully.

"We couldn't keep them all," O'Riain said. "They're in good homes - as long as the people don't get hunted out."

Risteard was bursting to hear Turlough's story. They sat together while Turlough recounted his adventures once more. Then he listened to Risteard's story of how they were ordered out of Cragg. The land was forfeit to the government and would be taken by Ironsides. Risteard shook as he recounted his sorrow at leaving the place where he had been so happy.

"But we'll go back, Eamon said. He said we'll go back." There were tears in his eyes and his mouth trembled.

"You will," Turlough patted him on the back.

O'Riain beckoned him to one side. "He's upset, the poor child," O'Riain said. "He can't talk about it - or about my mother."

"Your mother?"

O'Riain put his hand to his face. He took a deep breath.

"My poor mother, God be good to her. We were put out, as he told you. 'Twas too much for her. She's where she belongs, Lord have mercy on her, back home in Tipperary." He shuddered.

"I'm sorry," Turlough said.

"You know what 'tis like, my friend. When I met you first I didn't know the pain of it, old as I was, and you knew something that I didn't." His face twisted; then he smiled sadly and shook his head. "Changed times. There's not much safety in stopping with us. We're breaking up." He looked around sadly at his group.

"I've a horse now as well as a dog," Turlough pointed out.

"True. At least your feet will have some rest."

"I thank you for what you've done," Turlough said. "That's twice you've saved me."

"You shouldn't see them again. But there'll be other villains on your road so you must take care of yourself." He turned back to his men and shouted: "We'll have something to eat and then the lad's for the road again."

Turlough joined in the makeshift meal. Sitting beside him, Risteard chatted away about the fun he had had with Brian and David after Turlough left. But for all the laughter this was not like the meals they had shared in Cragg. The men were silent. They did not engage in the banter and teasing that had been common among them there, and which had made the meals at Cragg so much fun for himself and the boys.

There was little more to be said. He had his journey to make as they had theirs. When they had eaten O'Riain and his men stood around, waiting for him to start on his way. Bran Óg seemed impatient also, as he ran around among the men, barking at them in his own form of farewell. Turlough mounted. He nodded to Risteard. The small boy's eyes were once more full of tears. Each of his friends wished him well in turn, and with a wave Turlough bade them farewell and resumed his journey.

He noticed now that the appearance of the countryside was changing. Gone were the woods and hedges and in their place were stony, barren fields. This countryside was bereft of people to cultivate the land.

The miles slipped slowly away as they journeyed west. The horse slowed, travelling at little more than walking pace. From time to time Bran Óg took the lead.

Suddenly, Bran Óg gave a deep growl and his hair bristled. Turlough pulled up the horse and looked. Making their way around the bend of the road ahead two riders came into view. Horses and riders could not have been more unlike. One was a big hunter ridden by a thick-set, powerful soldier; the other was the feeblest-looking animal Turlough had ever seen. Even the worst garran at Ballinasloe was superior to such a beast. But if the wretched animal was worthy of note, its rider was even more so. Sitting astride the beast, his feet just off the ground, was a long lean man clothed in rags. His hands were tied; a rope encircled his shoulders. His face was the fresh, unlined face of a young man but his head was bald on top, surrounded by white hair which fell to his shoulders. A wispy white beard straggled from his chin.

There was no chance to get off the track and find cover. Turlough, with a calmness that came, he knew, from utter weariness, sat astride his horse and waited.

When they came up to him the soldier nudged his horse forward and stared at Turlough coldly. "Boy," he commanded, "what brings you here?"

Turlough glanced away from him. The soldier guided his horse between Turlough and the pony.

"Are you dumb?"

Turlough said nothing.

"Are you Papist?"

He pulled his sword and held it against Turlough's chest.

"Dismount," he ordered.

Turlough obeyed. The soldier jumped from his horse and stood towering over the young boy.

Suddenly, Bran Óg darted between his master and his adversary. The soldier stepped back in surprise. Turlough picked up a stone. Sword thrust out, the soldier darted forward.

He stopped short at the growl from the dog. The hair on the nape of Bran Óg's neck stood up stiffly; his teeth were bared and his eyes set on the big man. Snarling like a demon, Bran Óg launched himself at the soldier's sword-hand and bit deep. The soldier screamed and was forced to release his sword. Blood oozed from his hand. Bran Óg snatched at his hands as the soldier scrabbled to pick his sword off the ground.

Keeping his eye on the fight before him Turlough pulled his catapult from his belt and fixed a stone into the sling. The enraged soldier cursed and swore at Bran Óg. He took a grip of the hilt of the sword, swiping at Bran Óg with his free hand. Turlough took aim and fired for the soldier's face. As the stone shot forward, the soldier twisted to one side; the stone glanced off his helmet. Turlough snatched up another stone. With a furious oath the soldier rose to his feet, sword in hand. Bran Óg dived snarling at his ankles. The big man twisted round to strike at the dog. Turlough moved his position. He took aim and waited an instant.

"Bran!" Turlough shouted.

Bran Óg leapt back from the soldier.

Blood masking his cheek, the soldier turned round to face Turlough. Turlough shot. The stone caught the man dead centre in the forehead. His face turned white, his legs crumpled and he crashed to the ground.

Bran Óg gave a short whimper and sniffed at his stricken opponent.

"Release me, young man," the man on the garran pleaded.

Turlough looked at him uncertainly.

The tethered man sighed. "You don't trust me," he said.

When Turlough stayed silent he said gently, "He was your enemy, young man, as he was mine. I'm no danger to you."

His voice was soft and soothing. Like his face, it belonged to a young man. His pale blue eyes seemed to look into Turlough's mind.

Turlough undid the ropes around his shoulders and then untied his hands. The long man swung his leg across his horse's head and stood up unsteadily. He grasped Turlough by both hands and shook them with delight.

"A thousand thanks, my young hero. You saved my life," he said.

Still Turlough could not speak. The unexpected violence had left him dazed. Bran Óg, the real hero, Turlough thought, lay panting on the road.

They looked down at the soldier, motionless on the ground. The white-haired man knelt and placed his fingers against the soldier's neck.

"He'll not bother anyone for a long time," he sounded satisfied. "You and I will do well not to be here when he comes alive again. Let us take to the road and put as many miles as we can between us and him."

They looked at their mounts.

"I think mine deserves a rest," the old man said. "If you have no objection, my friend, I'll take possession of this fine animal, at least for a time." When Turlough nodded, he mounted the soldier's horse and took up the reins of his own worn-out mount. They rode away from their prostrate enemy.

"Who are you?" Turlough finally asked.

The old man smiled. "My fullest apology, my young saviour. I am Terence Rhattican, the Bard of Oranmore." He leaned over and shook hands solemnly with Turlough.

"What were you doing with the soldier?"

"That brute took it into his ignorant skull that I was a priest in disguise and was taking me where he was to collect a bounty and I would collect a hangman's noose." He paused for a moment. "Or maybe a passage to a foreign climate to work as a slave. I hear they do that to priests too in these stirring times."

Turlough thought of the Mass in the field at Dromineer. What had been that priest's fate? Images of his father and mother, too, edged into his mind.

Rhattican leaned over and patted him on the back. "Ah, my young friend," he said gently.

The kindness in Rhattican's voice prompted more memories. Turlough thought of Uncle Seán and of McNamara at Garykennedy. Pain and gratitude welled inside his chest. He was overwhelmed with tiredness and wished that he could find someplace where he could sleep in comfort and hold these precious memories tightly to himself.

But this was no time for such thought. He looked at Rhattican. These were dangerous times for men of God. But this man, he was not a priest.

"How did he mistake you for a priest?" Turlough asked.

Rhattican spoke softly. He had been sitting in his hut the previous night, reading his book by the light of a candle when the soldier burst in upon him. A man reading was an unusual sight in Ireland. Only educated men could read and, the soldier decided, only priests were educated men. "Therefore," Rhattican said with a wry smile, "I was a priest and fit only for the gallows. So here I am and I owe you my life. Whatever I can do for you, it will be done. But you tell me nothing of yourself. Why is such a young person on the road on his own?"

"I journey to relations."

"Where?"

"Mayo."

"You ride to Mayo?"

"If that is the best way to get there."

"A dangerous journey, young man, for a young person alone. Fraught with perils. There is another way and I can help you."

Turlough tensed. How could there be another way?

"I owe you my life. I have friends who can help. The sea is your way."

"The sea?"

"What is the sea but a road, and what is a ship but a vehicle for transport! Galway is a crossroads to the sea. My friends in the Claddagh will help any friend of mine." He smiled at Turlough. "My task now is to see you to Mayo."

Turlough began to protest but Rhattican silenced him with a wave of his hand.

"I have a debt to pay. I will pay it," he announced. "There is nothing more to be said."

XXI

"Do you know these parts well?" Turlough asked.

"Like my whiskers," the bard replied. "I know every blade of grass from here to Galway."

He started to sing but it was not a happy song. It was quiet and doleful, sung almost under his breath so that Turlough could not make out the words. He could only understand the sad tone. When the song stopped there was silence for a time, a quietness that was not even broken by the sounds of the birds.

Rhattican spoke. "I was thinking a strange thought: I know of no young poets."

"Where are they?"

"They are not in it. We are all old, the ones I know. When I was a young poet I knew many like myself. But now, there are no young ones. Where will the next of them come from?" His face was sombre. "And when the bards and the poets are gone, the stories and poetry will be gone. The history is gone then: there is nothing to keep it, to hand it down from day to day and year to year, from one generation to another. We are a lost people." He looked over Turlough's head, his eyes scanning the landscape. "We are a lost people then," he repeated.

He spoke no more for the remainder of that day's journey. As darkness fell they found shelter in a *bothán*. Rhattican crooned more sad songs to himself when they had eaten their meagre supplies.

"A bleak place this," Rhattican said, "that has no store of berries or herbs to sweeten a person's journey." He blessed himself and prayed quietly.

Turlough followed his example and then stretched out. Bran Óg had already put his head down to rest.

Turlough dreamed of his fight with the soldier. In his dream the soldier did not lose his sword. He held on to it and he did not fall to the stone. Instead he held the sword to Turlough's breast and, eyes cold as ice, stabbed him with it. As the sword entered his body Turlough woke up. Sweat rolled down his neck and chest. He was unable to return to sleep. He lay there for the rest of the night, listening to the rhythmic rise and fall of Bran Óg's breathing and the gentle snoring of the bard, trying to shut the horrible images out of his mind.

The bard woke at dawn. He started the morning with a prayer, then went outside. "A mighty morning," he shouted, rubbing his hand against the morning cold as he returned. "I slept with a clean conscience."

"How far are we from Galway?"

"Maybe a day's ride on the two garrans we have. Only one of us can straddle the soldier's horse. Today that is your privilege."

He would not hear of Turlough's objections, but watched beaming while Turlough mounted the great horse. Turlough looked down nervously. This horse was so much bigger and more powerful than his own.

"Never fear, my friend, he's trained to accept his rider. Have no fear," he encouraged as he straddled his own sad animal. His feet almost scraped the ground and his mount looked around sorrowfully before he reluctantly began to move.

That evening found them on the outskirts of Galway. Rhattican dismounted and signalled Turlough to do the same.

"We cannot ride this fine beast into the city. A soldier will recognise it as an army horse. But the saddle we can take with us. Or do you prefer to leave it aboard this happy beast to which we are giving freedom?"

"It's too heavy to carry."

"Indeed. But could it not be converted into cash money?" He winked at Turlough. "Would cash money go astray to either one of us, my young friend? There's many will see this saddle as a bargain if the money is right."

"We can sell it if you like," Turlough said.

"If I like?" Rhattican was indignant. "If there is cash money to be made from this saddle it is nothing to do with me. The money is yours alone."

"We can share ..."

"No," Rhattican said. "That cannot be. To the victor the spoils. These are the spoils of war and they belong to you. Do you not need cash money, young fellow?" he asked suddenly. "Do you maybe not know what cash money is?"

"I do."

"Do you indeed? In my experience it isn't many a young lad of your years that would know of it." Rhattican lowered the saddle towards the ground, then thought better of it and lifted it up again. His beard sank into the saddle and for a moment he lowered his cheek to it and rubbed it along the leather, sniffing as he did so.

"I have seen it," Turlough said.

"Where?"

"With my father."

"Aye. A good father will leave his son cash money," Rhattican said so softly he might have been speaking to himself.

"I didn't say he left it to me."

"And I didn't say that you did say so. I said that it was a good father that left his son cash money. My own father strove to do so but luck was not with him."

"You have the saddle."

Rhattican rubbed it against his cheek again. "I will carry this saddle to Galway and we will see if there are any who will pay cash for it." He swung the saddle onto the back of his garran. The soldier's horse wandered away from them and began to chomp the grass. Turlough picked up the reins of their two beasts and led them onward. Rhattican strode ahead without a backward glance.

Turlough could not help reflecting that the tall bard, striding through the streets of Galway, followed by a boy with two horses, one an old garran with two saddles, was not a sight which could easily be missed. Yet as they moved through the crowded streets, nobody gave them a second glance.

Turlough had to trot to keep pace with the bard who moved with surprising speed. Bran Óg darted round, drawn hither and thither by the curiosity of new smells.

"Where are we making for?" Turlough, gasping for breath, called to Rhattican.

"The Claddagh. My old friend O'Flaherty lives there among the fisherfolk."

They walked along the shoreline moving west from the city. It was a short distance, no more than a quarter of a mile, all the while in sight of the ocean.

"The broad Atlantic ocean, young fellow," Rhattican shouted back over his shoulder, waving his arm at the Atlantic as though it was a present which he wished to hand to his young friend. "Feast your eyes on it." He paused for a moment and then frowned. "No. You have seen it in your years at Coonagh. This is nothing new to you." He sounded disappointed.

They made their way through twisting streets, filled with fishing cots and crowded with people. It was as if they had entered another town. The men were dressed in the well-worn clothes of working fishermen. The women wore blue mantles and red skirts, and their heads were covered with bright red cloth.

A crock of dirty water thrown out of a cot landed across Bran Óg. He stopped with a yelp. Looking disconsolately at the offending doorway, he stood and shook himself. Rhattican laughed at the sight of his distress, then drew Turlough's attention to the work the people of the Claddagh were engaged in. The fish had all been landed and families worked together preparing it for the market. Every member of the family worked without pause.

"All caught in Galway Bay, right there in front of you," Rhattican shouted to him above the noise of the workers. "All God's plenty of fish. Much more than you'll find in Coonagh on the Shannon," he teased. "Here you'll get turbot even a brace of Tipperary farmers would be hard put to eat for their dinner; cod, sole, hake, haddock, ling, pollock both black and white, bream, mullet, mackerel and eel. And then you'll have crabs, lobsters, crayfish, oysters, shrimps, cockles and mussels."

Turlough looked around with awe. He could believe that such a variety was possible from what he saw before him.

"And the king of them all - the sun-fish," Rhattican said, his voice falling in wonder.

"Where is it?"

"Ah, maybe not here now, but it is known."

"What is it?" Turlough asked.

"Aha," Rhattican called out triumphantly. "I thought you wouldn't know, coming from Coonagh. The sun-fish or basking shark, young fellow, for which any man here will risk his life, is so bountiful it can set a fisherman up for the rest of the year. If he can bring it in." He shook his head slowly and smiled to himself.

"Look." Rhattican stopped and caught Turlough by the shoulder. He pointed out the Bay, where one boat stood out from the others. It had a white sail and, by contrast, colours flew gaily from the masthead.

"Whose is it?"

"The Mayor of Claddagh. He is the law here. Not even the soldiers in Galway will come in here with their laws. They leave the people of Claddagh to their own ancient laws and know that no trouble will come of it."

"Why is that?"

"It's the way it is because it is the way it always has been. Anyway," he laughed, "the foreigners do not know these people's speech. Indeed, even the people of Galway cannot understand the Irish of these people."

Rhattican marched on. Turlough followed, treading in his wake, holding tightly to the reins. He kept an eye on Bran Óg, who was intent on sniffing every new smell. Even the fish, which he would never eat, he sniffed out of habit and curiosity.

"Here we are," Rhattican finally shouted to Turlough. He removed the extra saddle from the back of his old horse. "God bless all here," he greeted.

There was a murmur from within. He threw the saddle to the the ground just inside the door. Then he thrust the top part of his body into the gloom of the cot, resting against the top of the half-door.

"Come in, young fellow," he directed Turlough.

Turlough dropped the reins of the two beasts and cautioned Bran Óg to sit by the door.

A young woman in a shawl smiled as they entered. Rhattican had to stoop to fit into the low-roofed cabin and found it more comfortable to sit down. He leaned back against the wall with his long legs crooked in front of him. The young woman beckoned Turlough forward. She pointed to the table and indicated that he should help himself to some of the freshly baked bread. He spread butter across it and the butter slowly melted into the bread. It was warm, succulent, delicious.

"And where's himself, Nóirín?" Rhattican asked.

"Ah," she said with disgust, but laughing at the same time, "where do you think?"

Turlough found it hard to understand what she said. Her accent was very strange and her harsh voice was out of tune with her person. He listened more closely.

"At the wars again," the bard was saying, and winked.

"The wars, is it? The tavern, you mean, you long string of misery," she burst out and then broke into laughter. "Where you'll be with him soon, I don't doubt."

"And why is he not out there with you and his catch, sorting it like all those other good people?"

"Because he's rich," she cried out, laughing.

"Did he come into riches, the decent man?"

"He caught a sun-fish a month ago last Tuesday, so he's retired now to live on his wealth," she mocked.

"Well for him."

"Aye. He left the catches today to them that haven't his wealth."

"Decent man," Rhattican laughed back at her. "Turlough, Turlough, listen to this woman. Eyes that sparkle with the light of the sky on a clear morning in September, a skin as fresh as the flowers that bloom on the buds of May, a step as light as the butterfly in a July meadow. All these things," he paused and looked from Turlough to the woman.

Turlough saw that she was blushing as she waited for the bard to finish. Her eyebrows were raised expectantly; her lips quivered with a half-buried smile.

"And the tongue of a shrew," Rhattican finished with a bellow.

She burst out laughing and made to throw a piece of bread at him. "Go on," she said, "go on and find him."

"I will find him, Nóirin of the Shrewish Tongue, and bring that good man back to you, never fret."

"I don't fret," she said. "I know he'll come back. Doesn't he always know how to find his way home?"

"Has he any plans for taking to the sea?"

"Maybe he has, maybe he hasn't. A rich man can suit himself."

"Could he be persuaded to take my young friend and saviour

here up to the Mayo coast, I wonder?" Rhattican looked at her.

She shook her head. The bard's eyebrows flickered in surprised.

"And why not?"

"He's sworn an oath he'll let no boy aboard after the last one."

"What last one, woman? Will you stop talking in riddles."

"There's no riddle about it. Since you were last here yourself, some fool of a young fellow persuaded my man to take him aboard and the loodramawn fell over and was lost off Aran."

"God be good to him."

"And himself slept no wink of sleep for near half a year after."

"Did he know him?"

"He was no kin of ours, if that's what you mean."

"No. He has a soft heart."

"You'd best test that for yourself but I'll warrant he'll take no boy with him."

They stepped out of the cabin. The horses stood patiently waiting, surrounded by a group of small boys. Turlough ordered Bran Óg to stay.

"Will he take me?" Turlough asked.

"Maybe, maybe not. He is a stubborn man."

They entered the dockside. It was filled with boats and ships, and sailors dressed in strange garb moving to and fro.

Suddenly, so unexpectedly that Turlough bumped straight into his back, Rhattican halted. The bard placed a long thin hand on Turlough's chest as if to hold him back. "God help us," he said.

Turlough looked, following the direction of Rhattican's gaze. He saw a boat lying low in the water. Ascending the gangway were a string of boys, tethered by ropes, their ragged clothes fluttering in the breeze. A sailor drove them forward with a rope that he laid across their shoulders. His curses carried all over the docks. Crying and snuffling, the wretched boys climbed the gangway and stumbled aboard the boat.

Rhattican put a finger to his lips. He swung away from the cruel sight and steered Turlough swiftly across the dockside. But Turlough could not tear his eyes away; he looked back, his face ashen and cold. A small sailor leaned over the side, shouting to a mate. The sailor reminded him of Peadar. With a shudder he turned and followed Rhattican.

XXII

RHATTICAN LED the way, pushing boldly through the narrow crowded streets. They came to a stop in a street that seemed to be devoted to taverns, the inhabitants of which were mainly sailors. The bustle of activity was as great as elsewhere but Turlough noticed that there were no women or children here. Irish and English, and occasionally sounds that Turlough could not identify, rang along the cobblestones.

The bard swung off into a laneway and marched through the low doorway of a tavern. Inside it was dark. When his eyes became accustomed to the gloom Turlough was able to make out men sitting along a wall. Behind the counter stood a small, thin man with a handkerchief knotted on top of his head. He looked with distaste at Turlough. His expression changed when he saw Rhattican but before he could say anything the door swung open again and a group of sailors pushed their way inwards, stumbling and shouting at each other. One pushed against Rhattican who put out his long arm and gently held the offender at arm's length. The sailor opened his mouth to say something but found he had to lean back to look up at the bard's face, and then, thinking better of it, he shut his mouth with a snap. He lurched away to join his staggering companions.

The man behind the counter and Rhattican eyed each other warily.

"He's not here," the innkeeper said curtly.

"Did I ask for him?"

"Who else would you be looking for?"

"I might not be looking for anyone."

The innkeeper nodded at this and thought about it for a moment. "If you knew where he was you wouldn't be here," he said after a pause. "Why else would you leave the drinking shops of the Claddagh to come into the city, unless he broke out from his woman and went roving up here?"

"You're a wise man," Rhattican said.

The other gave a sour smile.

"Take care a man as sharp as yourself does not cut himself," Rhattican said softly, turning for the door.

As they reached the door there was the sound of shouting from the back of the gloomy den. A table turned over with a crash. Rhattican and Turlough paused at the exit to look back. Two sailors, their faces snarling, were fighting. Suddenly one of the pair screamed and twisted away, scrambling for the doorway. Turlough stood back as the man staggered out, holding his side. The man's eyes were glazed over as he lurched into the street.

"Quickly, young fellow," Rhattican hissed and pulled Turlough after him. They dashed into the street, nearly stumbling over the wounded sailor stretched on the cobbles.

"Don't wait, come," Rhattican ordered. They sprinted down the street. "This place will crawl with soldiers; no time to waste." They didn't pause until they were at the bottom of the cobbled street. They turned the corner and the bard leaned against the wall to catch his breath.

"What a hell the world has turned into," he cried.

"Where do we go now?" Turlough asked.

"Our man is somewhere around here. He'll not be gone home yet."

He caught his breath with a gasp.

"And what have we here?" a harsh voice demanded.

Two soldiers, hands on swords, stood in front of them.

"Gentlemen," Rhattican said.

"Who are you?"

"A humble bard."

Turlough examined them. They were the same height, about middle size, and in their uniforms they looked the same as the soldier he had encountered only the day before. Again, they had the same pale expression and the same hard, unsmiling kind of face. They stood perfectly still, hands on their swords, waiting for the bard to say more. When he said nothing the first of them asked, "What is this 'bard'?"

"Me," Rhattican said, laughing.

They stared at him without expression.

"A humble maker of verses. A storyteller of sorts," he explained.

"Name of?" the second soldier asked.

"Terence Rhattican."

"From what place?"

"Oranmore."

"This isn't Oranmore," the first one pointed out.

"I have business ..."

"Where?"

"The Claddagh."

"Then why aren't you there?"

"I have to make my way there," Rhattican said carefully.

"Poet," the second one said, spitting on the ground. "Is there anything else in this country save poets? Everywhere we go there is an infestation of poets and wordsmiths."

"And rebellious murderers," the first soldier snapped.

Rhattican's smile faded.

"The boy: name?"

"Turlough."

"My son," Rhattican murmured.

"Son?" said the soldier. "Grandson, you mean."

"No. Son," Rhattican insisted.

"You are too old, old man," the first one said, his knuckles white as he gripped his sword.

"Gentlemen, I assure you. I was not blessed with a child until old with years."

"How old?"

"Sixtieth birthday."

The second soldier gave a raucous laugh. "Indeed," he sneered. "And your wife?"

"A young woman, alas, not destined long for this world. She died in childbirth."

"No doubt she saw the whelp and died of fright," the soldier nudged his companion.

"Or woke up to see what she had married to become the father of her brat," the other said and both laughed loudly.

They watched Rhattican closely as they laughed. Turlough could feel the danger in the air. Their cold eyes never left the bard's face. Then, slowly, Rhattican's face creased into a smile, small at first but it grew until he was grinning like a half-wit. Still they watched him as if this was the first time they had ever seen anyone laugh. Then, as abruptly as they had accosted Turlough and Rhattican, they turned on their heels and stalked away.

Rhattican stared after them. His mouth still held a smile but, Turlough saw, his eyes were hard.

"Come on, young fellow," he said, and they made their way into an alley.

This one was empty; in the quiet their footsteps fell heavily on the cobbles. There was a quick noise, a swish, and before Turlough could cry out Rhattican had fallen over and was on his back. His head struck off the cobblestones with a crack that made Turlough wince. He lay still. Turlough's attempt to move was strangled as a hand was clamped on his mouth. From the corner of his eye he saw that a whip lay curled around the bard's legs and, with an inward groan, he knew who held it.

XXIII

PEADAR STRUTTED forward, gathering up his whip as he came towards Turlough. He jerked on the whip and the line around Rhattican's legs uncurled. Peadar looked down with a smile at the bard's prone body. He licked his lips in satisfaction.

Turlough struggled to breathe against the hand across his mouth.

"Now, boy," Peadar said, "when my nephew is good enough to let you go, remember this: one sound and he will break your neck. Do you understand this?"

Turlough felt the pressure around his mouth increasing as the grip tightened. He tried to nod but he couldn't. Peadar nodded. The hand across his mouth slowly relaxed and he was released.

"Old friends cannot be parted for long," Peadar snarled. "I had a feeling we'd meet again. But I'm afraid this will be for the last time."

He looked down at Rhattican who lay unconscious on the cobbled street.

"You know, you have a knack for picking big friends."

"Is he dead?" Shane asked.

Peadar shrugged. "Leave him. Our young friend here is what we want."

Turlough looked around in desperation. The lane was empty.

"We're in the right place to put an end to your adventures, boy. We have a friend with a boat full of boys. He's going on an adventure across the Atlantic ocean to foreign parts, and a berth can be found for you, I'm delighted to say. Then we'll be a few crowns the richer."

"Cut his throat and be done with it," Shane growled, looking anxiously down the lane.

"No! There's business to be done here and a crown or two to

be turned. I won't have sentiment interfere with business!"

"And what about Murty? Buried in the side of a ditch, all over this whelp," Shane hissed at his uncle.

Peadar was about to answer but stiffened as two men came out of a tavern. They looked at the group gathered around the bard with astonishment. But they seemed to take notice only of Turlough and Peadar and Shane, and looked at them with curiosity.

But can they not see the bard? Turlough thought to himself. Are they blind?

They were drunk. The older one lurched back against the wall and studied the group. A broadly built man with a large stomach, he had powerful shoulders and descending from them a pair of arms that seemed too small for him. A pipe hung sideways from his mouth and across his forehead was a mark that might have been a tattoo. He grinned drunkenly.

"Stand easy," Peadar muttered to Shane, "and if this brat moves you can have your way – stick your *scian* into his ribs. You hear me, boy?"

Turlough nodded. Shane placed an arm casually across Turlough's shoulder.

The drunken pipe-smoker's companion was smaller and younger. His broad smile showed white even teeth set against his weather-beaten face. He staggered, too, and said something to his friend. They pointed at the bard's body and giggled loudly.

"Friends," the man with the pipe called. "We're all in the one boat, eh? Too much cargo on board. Weighed down by ballast, eh?" He roared with drunken laughter.

Peadar laughed back at them and waited as they staggered forward.

"And the boy – is he the worse for drink too, eh?" the big man asked. "He needs whipping being drunk at his age."

"Worry not, friend, he'll get the whipping of his life when we fetch him home," Peadar said, eyeing the big man with caution.

By now the two drunkards were standing over Rhattican. They looked up from his body, their faces a mixture of curiosity and disgust. The big one, his pipe still hanging shakily from his mouth, muttered something to his companion and then looked sharply at Peadar.

"Such a to-do," he said, shaking his head. "Such a to-do and at his age, too. Has he no shame? An old man that should be at home; at home, I say, saying his prayers and preparing to meet his maker, instead of lying around in gutters, making a spectacle of himself for strangers, and then falling down dead drunk into the street. I never saw the like of this before, friend, eh? Not your father, friend?"

Peadar quickly shook his head. "We're strangers here. We came upon him this instant. I'd say he had too much drink and fell over himself."

Turlough tensed but felt the edge of Shane's dagger against his back. He expelled his breath slowly, and watched helplessly as the two men pulled the bard upright.

"We'll not leave the drunken brute here," the older man said. "'Twouldn't be Christian. We'll find him a berth somewhere."

One stood on each side of the unconscious Rhattican, propping him up.

"Good day to you, gentlemen," Peadar said jovially as they shuffled past.

The men did not look back. "Good day to you," a voice called out and they disappeared around the corner of the lane.

Peadar and Shane grabbed Turlough and turned down the laneway. They looked to either side and then, holding him by the arms, they propelled him through the streets at a hectic pace. A terrible fear took possession of Turlough. This was the end, for he knew that they were making their way to the boat on the dockside. He had endured so much for this!

He fought against his fear, willing himself to find some means of escape. But even while he thought of it he knew that there was none. Either one of his captors would kill him before they let him escape again, and in this town of strangers there was no one to help him. His one friend could not know where he was. And he had left Bran Óg behind in the Claddagh.

They had reached the docks. Turlough saw the boat onto which the boys had earlier been herded. There were no boys there now.

"Hold him fast," Peadar ordered. He called out to the boat and stood back as Shane marched Turlough along the gangway.

The man who greeted them was big and weather-beaten with dark, almost black eyes. He looked the three of them over in silence. His air of menace and power reminded Turlough of Ireton at Limerick; the same sort of cold presence that exuded a cruel authority. This man dominated lives.

"A new one," Peadar said.

"I have enough."

"Look," Shane said. He slapped Turlough across the chest with the flat of his hand. "Sound of wind and limb. About twelve and look at the size of him. He's nearly a full grown man already."

"Look at the puny specimens the rest of them are," Peadar said in a cajoling tone. "This one is worth any three of the others you have there. By the time this one is sixteen he'll work harder than any full grown man on any of your foreign plantations."

Turlough's attention was suddenly caught by a strange sight at the prow. A black man! A large muscular man coloured black from head to toe was leaning over the side, shouting instructions to someone below. The black man's teeth gleamed as he spoke. His face was the colour of mahogany.

Turlough felt his right arm being lifted. Shane held it forward for the master's inspection. "Feel the muscle there," he invited.

The master of the boat looked at Shane with distaste.

"Usual price," he snapped.

Peadar and Shane looked at one other. Each waited for the other to speak.

"Are you coming with us too?" the master looked at them cooly. "It's the usual price. I have a tide to catch to make my rendezvous." He turned away. "Stow him below with the others," he called back over his shoulder.

A few planks were hauled aside to reveal a large hold. The two men caught Turlough by the wrists and twisted them viciously behind his back. Turlough screamed. He was caught by the hair and dragged across the deck to the hold. He dropped into total darkness.

As he came to he gagged at the smell. He moved his head from side to side slowly, trying to shake loose the cloud that hung round his head. His stomach heaved: the stench was unbearable. Not since the worst days of the pestilence in Limerick had he known anything so obnoxious. He vomited.

All around deathly pale faces were staring at him. The hold of the boat was a prison – a prison for boys like Turlough. No one spoke. The sense of despair and desolation was palpable. Then there was a cough, a low chesty cough.

Turlough heard the cough and looked around. He could barely see the figure that was bent over, his body shaking. Slowly the coughing subsided. The boy straightened up.

"What's your name?" he asked.

"Turlough."

"Liam," he said. He indicated that Turlough should move back beside him.

Turlough crawled over the wet slippery boards. He hardened himself, disgusted, as he recognised the source of the dreadful smell – the boards were covered in scraps of rotting food, water and dirt. Some of the boys had been stuck in this damp, airless hole for days. Liam moved slightly to make room for him.

To have made it this far and be condemned to slavery! Now the Bay and the Holy Mountain were lost to him. Turlough hid his face in his hands. So many times before there had been dark and dismal days, but he had survived.

Liam shook his arm. "He's Donnchadha from Athenry," he said, referring to the boy on the other side of Turlough.

"How many of us are in it?" Turlough asked.

"You make thirteen," Liam said, laughing bitterly.

"Where are we bound for?"

"No one knows except bits and pieces of information from listening to them above." Liam indicated the deck overhead. "We think this boat is to sail out to meet up with a ship bound across the ocean."

"Where do you come from?" Donnchadha asked.

"Limerick."

"Who caught you?"

"A pair from Roscommon. Who caught you?"

"A soldier," Liam answered first. "The masters of boats like these have agents everywhere. There's nowhere safe."

"I was snatched from my father minding horses at Ballinasloe," Donnchadha said sadly.

"Shush," a nearby figure admonished. "Don't say too much. We're down but don't lose heart yet."

From his voice and outline Turlough judged that the speaker was older and bigger than the rest of them. There was a sense of purpose in his tone. "That's Seán," Liam told him.

"From Galway itself," Seán said. "An orphan of the war. While we're still here we have some hope. Now, I say we have no more talk. These planks have ears."

An eerie silence descended on the black hole, the only sound the straining of the ropes which held the boat. A long time passed in the darkness, and then a shower of light filled the hold as two planks were pulled aside overhead. A few buckets were lowered on ropes. The sight of the buckets was the signal for a hectic scramble.

"Easy," Seán called out. "Remember yesterday. Easy, and we'll all get a bit."

"One of the buckets spilled out on the floor," Liam explained. "That left us hungry, I can tell you."

The buckets were passed around. The contents, a thin gruel, had a nauseating taste which Turlough could not force down.

"I know," Donnchadha said, "but when it's all you'll get, you can be grateful even for this."

The buckets were taken up, the planks restored and a fitful calm returned to the dark hold. The little light filtering through began to die and the hold grew black as pitch. The darker it became the more obnoxious grew the smell.

"Try and sleep," Seán advised Turlough. "Tomorrow's a new day and you never know what it might bring."

But Turlough could not sleep, and neither could many of his companions. Some wept, others cried out in nightmares. There was the sound, too, of persistent coughing from the boys lying in the cold and damp of their prison.

As the first streaks of light squeezed into the hold there were sounds of activity on deck. Muffled noises echoed through the hold; voices could be heard on top. Turlough froze: the motion of the boat had changed. Beside him Liam and Donnchadha were also alert.

"We're off to sea," Seán said grimly.

XXIV

THE PLANKS covering the hatch were pulled away, blinding the boys with light so that they had to screw up their eyes to look at the figure standing at the opening. A pole was lowered in to the hold and the black man climbed half-way down.

"Listen to me carefully. I will not repeat this." He had a deep voice and he spoke his words slowly and with care. "We are away from land on the high seas. You are to come up onto the deck. We do not want you dead before we take you to your new homes. There you will have sunlight, at least, instead of the rain that marks the Irish summer. Now: if you attempt to do anything that is foolish when you are on deck, I will throw you overboard for the shark. I will do this myself even if I do not want you dead. Am I understood?" He looked at them without expression.

The idea of being in the fresh air took possession of the boys; they shouted and started to move. They were stopped by a roar from the black man. "You have been warned," he said. "There will be no rush forward. You will come in single file. Those who are nearest come first."

The boys nearest the pole moved forward hesitantly; each of the captives followed.

As he came out on deck Turlough looked around. Immediately his glance fell on Peadar and Shane. Somehow they no longer seemed so threatening, even though Turlough was a captive and soon to be a slave thanks to them. They leered at him, but at the same time their faces were unusually pale, their expressions uneasy.

The craft seemed even smaller now than when he had seen it at the docks. It had one sail, dirty brown in colour and showing signs of wear and tear. He studied the boat in dismay. How could a boat of this size cross into the swells and storms of the great Atlantic ocean? He had heard enough stories from friends of his father's who had been in these waters to know that they were treacherous. This was not a ship to hold its own against the power of great seas.

"Stand together," the master ordered. A crewman nearby held a musket on them. "Tie them," he ordered the black man.

Eyes fixed on the master, each boy stood still as the black man roughly tied their hands behind their backs.

"Any of you making a sudden move is fish-bait," the master said and turned away.

A fresh wind was blowing but their vessel was making slow progress in the seas. The boys had been in the hold in cramped conditions for so long that it was a luxury to walk the deck, even bound as they were. They held their heads back and took in deep breaths of the tangy sea air. But those who were suffering worst from being held below decks coughed hard as they drew in the salty air, and the rolling of the boat did not agree with some who were already leaning against the side of the ships, their eyes glazed.

Turlough was able to have a close look at his companions. Liam was a brown-haired boy with a pale, freckled face and his nose stuck out prominently. He was thin and bony. Seán, the oldest of them, was tall. He had broad shoulders and a deep chest, long arms and legs, but his clothes hung on him to suggest that he had once filled them more comfortably than he did now.

The land slipped slowly by, Clare to port and to starboard the stony face of Connemara. The fresh winds made for a choppy passage. For Turlough the movement of the boat was familiar; at times the Shannon estuary could be rough but that had never deterred his father or uncle when the fishing and netting were good. But by now sea-sickness had afflicted almost all of his companions and most of them were retching. With their hands tied behind their backs, their sickness was a pitiful sight.

The boat rolled heavily as Galway Bay widened and they drew closer to the full expanse of the Atlantic. The sickness did not abate for the sufferers: it became worse. The boys lay slumped against the side of the boat, their faces as gloomy as the clouds that scudded overhead. He noticed with glee that both Peadar and Shane, his tormentors, were doubled up in the throes of sickness, their faces now completely drained of colour.

Seán gave Turlough a sharp elbow in the side and nodded towards the stern. Turlough followed his glance. Two boats had appeared where a few minutes before there had been an empty bay. Turlough and Seán watched as slowly but surely the two boats gained on their vessel.

"Who can they be?" Turlough asked.

"These are O'Flaherty seas," Seán said, "and that could be as bad for us as it is for these slavers. Those hookers are from the Claddagh by the look of them."

Turlough looked more closely. Seán was right. One was flying the colours of the Mayor of Claddagh, which Rhattican had pointed out to him only the day before.

"The Mayor of Claddagh," Turlough said.

"Yes," Seán grinned. "Now these men will pay. If he thinks they have fished his waters, he will cut them to bits. No one fishes the traditional waters without the permission of the Mayor of Claddagh."

There was a roar from the master: he had spotted the advancing craft.

"We need more speed," the black man called to him.

The master looked up at his tattered sails and shook his head. There was no hope there.

Like spiders approaching a fly the two hookers closed steadily on the slavers. As they came up Turlough could make out some of the men on board the hookers. The figure at the helm seemed familiar, but he could not think where he had seen him before. He stared intently. It was the man who had picked Rhattican off the ground and helped him away; and there was the younger man also, at the stern of the craft, a grappling hook in his hand.

Turlough shook himself in bewilderment. Yes. Beside the blocky man at the helm was Bran Óg! "My dog!" he bellowed in Seán's ear.

"Thank God. We're among friends!" Seán cried.

Tack as he might the master could not escape his pursuers. One hundred yards separated them and Turlough and the boys watched in fascination as the distance closed even further. The young man that Turlough recognised was at the prow readying his grappling iron. He threw it. It caught.

All thoughts of escape by the crew of the slaver had faded; now it was a question of survival.

The Claddagh men quickly boarded the slaver. The master had abandoned his post at the tiller and stood at the ready, his musket aimed at the nearest invader. He fired but a lurch of the boat spoiled his aim; he threw the gun down with an oath and unsheathed his sword. At his shoulder stood his black mate; the crewmen, too, stiffened themselves for combat. Bunched together they held off three of the Claddagh men, but sailors from the second boat were ready to come on board. Peadar and Shane, once so fearsome, cowered at the bow.

Turlough saw a familiar figure transferring unsteadily from the Mayor's boat. The long lean figure of Rhattican was unmistakable.

A little ball of lightning ran across the deck, barking for dear life, and aimed itself at Turlough. With his arms still tied behind his back Turlough caught the full force of the dog in his midriff, and bent double. He was blinded as Bran Óg licked his face. Gasping, Turlough straightened. "Bran Óg, you're more trouble than you're worth!" he exclaimed, laughing through the pain in his stomach. Cheers of joy began to ring round the boat as the boys' hands were untied by the Claddagh men. Turlough's hands were quickly freed. He looked around for Rhattican.

Rhattican was at the gunwhale opposite, on the edge of the fighting, holding a sword warily in his hand. He seemed to have little use for it, as the Claddagh men outnumbered the slavers and steadily beat them back.

Suddenly the master of the boat broke from the cluster of struggling men and dashed for the side. Rhattican, standing uncertainly, barred his way. With an oath the master swung his weapon and swept the sword out of the bard's grip. "I'll have you anyway!" he roared, raising his blade to bring the fatal blow down on Rhattican's head.

"No!" Turlough screamed and in a blur of movement he was across the deck and launched himself at the master's sword arm. He hit against the master's side, deflected the blow as it fell. A searing pain burned his shoulder. He crumpled on the deck.

"You whelp!" the slaver drew back his arm to strike again.

He stopped dead, an expression of disbelief crossing his face. His knees buckled and he slumped to the ground.

Fineen O'Flaherty walked from behind the slave-master. Shaking his head, he reached down and removed his boat-hook from the dead man's back. The fighting was over.

Slowly, unsteadily, Turlough and Rhattican helped one another to their feet. Rhattican looked at Turlough's wounded arm. "You will be fine, my young friend," Rhattican said softly. "You will be fine."

"The courage of a sun-fish," O'Flaherty's voice rang with admiration.

"To the victor, the spoils," Rhattican shouted, holding

Turlough's good arm in the air. "Fineen O'Flaherty, meet the saviour of my life."

The blocky captain of the Claddagh hooker smiled and shook Turlough's hand. "A good turn deserves a good turn," he said. "A friend of Rhattican is a friend of mine."

"Turlough, Fineen O'Flaherty, captain of the Galway seas," Rhattican pronounced with great solemnity.

"Where are the others?" Turlough asked.

"Two battered seamen, two cowardly wretches, and one bruised man of dark hue – in the hold," a Claddagh man announced.

"Bring them up," O'Flaherty directed his men. "They can have this cursed vessel because they will never darken Galway Bay again. The cursed priest-hunters will forever wander the seas without a moment's peace." He turned to Turlough. "The Mayor's boat will take your young friends back to Galway."

Turlough nodded with satisfaction.

"And you – you I will take to Mayo personally."

"Your journey is almost completed, my young friend," Rhattican said.

Turlough grimaced and held on to Bran Óg. He had heard Rhattican say that before!

XXV

THEY TRANSFERRED the boys to the Mayor's boat and waved farewell. Fineen O'Flaherty, Rhattican and Turlough watched as the slaver sailed off with its melancholy crew, none more miserable than Peadar and Shane. Fineen told his men to make sail.

"This old man here," O'Flaherty raised his voice, punching Rhattican in the ribs, "had us out scouring Galway last night. Nary a sign of you anywhere, but then we thought of the boat."

"Why didn't you come last night?" Turlough asked Rhattican.

"These men are good fighters on land, my friend, but on water they are the equal of any pirate that ever sailed the ocean! They knew that this tub would be no match for their craft and, anyway, the open sea can tell no tales."

O'Flaherty threw his hands in the air. "Such a liar!" he cried out to the sea. "A poet and a liar."

"Are you not the lucky man now to meet me as I was the lucky man to meet you?" Rhattican said to Turlough. "This O'Flaherty will take you on the last part of your journey."

Bran Óg gave a bark of delight.

"He knows, the creature," Rhattican laughed.

O'Flaherty ran his hand across Bran Óg's back. "He's as wise as yourself," he said to Rhattican, winking at Turlough. "Look at him, the broken-down old man. A mighty storyteller, though, and as good a poet as you'll meet. He's been singing your praises and telling us of your exploits on the road to Galway."

"Will you stop your rambling!" Rhattican shouted in exasperation.

"Enough so," O'Flaherty said agreeably. "We've a fair wind and an eager crew, so let us make sail for the Bay of Islands." He turned to Rhattican. "Did you tell him?"

"No. You tell him."

Turlough felt a stab of anxiety as he heard the men's tone.

"We have to tell you that we're going into dangerous waters. Not the waters themselves, but the people who sail them. The O'Malleys do not take kindly to foreign ships."

"Foreign!"

"Any ship that is not their own, they regard as a foreigner in their waters." O'Flaherty shrugged. "In the Claddagh, we don't take kindly to strangers fishing our waters either. The O'Malleys are the same."

"We can explain to them," Turlough protested.

O'Flaherty gave a hard laugh. "Of course we can. You can explain to a cannonball?"

Turlough looked at him in amazement.

"The O'Malleys have cannon. They have had cannon since the great Granuaile governed that coast. They may fire at us first and ask their questions after. We do not know. This is not a big ship, but it will make a good target for an O'Malley."

"You will risk it?" Rhattican queried.

"Of course I'll risk it. An O'Flaherty is not to be put to shame by an O'Malley."

"They are Turlough's people," Rhattican pointed out.

"And good people. But hasty. I can be hasty, too: we will take our boat on and see what is to come." He walked away to speak to his helmsman.

"Is he putting his boat in danger?" Turlough asked Rhattican.

"Him? Even if they spot us, they can see with their eye-glass that we are no danger to them. And even if they see us as a danger, our gallant captain can leave the big ships of the O'Malleys in his wake. Even the pirates of Mayo respect this one." Rhattican looked out at the open sea.

Turlough turned to the sea also. He felt tension and excitement grow in him now as he entered on the last lap of his journey. He thought of his fellow captives on their way back to Galway, returning to their families. What lay ahead of him at the end of this journey? Turlough sighed. Until now his whole concern had been to get here, to break free from the horrors of Limerick. What would he find in Mayo? Would it be like his mother's stories? Her father had died, he knew, but her mother – his grandmother – was alive. Or had been. And there were his mother's brothers and sisters and their children, his cousins.

His thoughts were broken by a nudge from O'Flaherty. "Here, lad, take this," he pushed a wedge of bread and butter into his fist, followed by a bowl of milk. "The woman thought you'd not be too well fed in your last berth."

Turlough picked at the edge of the bread, his mind still held by thoughts of the future. Bran Óg looked up at him with pleading eyes and Turlough offered him the slice. He watched the dog fondly as he gulped the bread: Bran Óg had followed loyally, through good times and bad. Turlough sipped the milk, then let the bowl down on the deck for Bran Óg to finish.

He made his way to the stern and sat beside Rhattican. They leaned against the gunwhales and admired the skill with which O'Flaherty handled the hooker. Answering every subtle change of wind, the sail was constantly trimmed and the tiller kept under a firm hand. The little craft slipped through the water.

Soon the islands of Aran dominated the sea. Rhattican was a fund of knowledge as he related the lore of the islands – Mór, Meán and Thiar – the Magical Islands of the West.

"Some day you should visit the big island, Inish Mór," he said to Turlough, "and take yourself up to Dún Aengus."

"What is Dún Aengus?"

"A great stone fort. It has been there on the island since the beginning of time. But," he smiled, "they tell a great many tales on those islands, too; enough to keep a young fellow listening for a month. No: for a year!"

"What kind of stories?"

"Did you never hear tell of Oisín?" the bard asked in astonishment.

"Of course I did. Oisín and Niamh Cinn Óir and the Fairy Islands. My mother told me all those stories."

"The very ones. Your mother was a clever woman. There they are," Rhattican pointed to the steep cliff of the island they were approaching. "Up there on the Dún they lived. Some day, take a journey up there for yourself – you will never forget it. And maybe you will meet the wanderer Oisín. He is a wanderer like yourself, you know!"

He caught Turlough urgently by the shoulder and pointed across to the mainland. "Over there – the world you belong to. But keep in mind the place you see here: this is where there is peace."

"Why?" quizzed Turlough.

"Whatever happens on land – war, Ironsides or slavers – no matter what it is, none of it will come here. They will leave the people of the islands alone."

"How do you know that?" Turlough asked.

"I know," Rhattican said solemnly, "and you remember it too, because some day it may stand you in good stead. The people here are not like any other people in Ireland, and somehow I'm sure the Sassanach know it."

By now they had left the shelter of the islands and were moving swiftly through the open sea. Turlough looked back at Aran until it was lost in the haze. He heard the cries of seagulls shrieking and whirling as they plummeted from the sky.

"How long?" he asked Rhattican.

"Long enough yet," the bard replied, and fell silent.

The distant landscape changed, mountains dominating the land that Rhattican called Connemara. As they sailed northwards the hills ranged to the starboard side, but as the day slipped past noon the mountains fell astern. Bran Óg lay contentedly at Turlough's feet. He would stir from time to time, stretch lazily, shake himself, and then flop down for another snooze.

Turlough was brought to life by a shout from O'Flaherty.

"There's your coast of Mayo, God help us," he laughed. "Keep an eye to the north-east there and soon enough you'll see your ancestral mountain."

"Where?"

"Clare Island."

A flood of memories raced into his mind.

"You won't see it for a while yet but when you do you can say you're at home."

But hours passed before Rhattican's hand on his shoulder told him to look again. He saw a big island which separated from the main bulk of the land as they made their way towards it under a favourable wind. His heart began to thump.

"In a moment you'll see your mountain," Fineen roared, waving his hand as if he was himself causing the mountain to appear.

There it was – the Holy Mountain! He saw it towering into the sky, its peak cradled with clouds, the mountain where St Patrick had fasted for forty days and nights.

"You're home," Rhattican clapped him across the back.

Turlough felt his eyes fill with tears. He moved away from Rhattican, wanting to be on his own at this moment. He took Bran Óg in his arms and pointed him to the mountain. "Home," he said under breath.

They skirted Clare Island and sailed on into the Bay. They were soon almost level with the mountain. The inlet was dotted with islands, more than he could count. This was the Bay of Islands.

"Steady," Fineen roared at his helmsman.

Turlough looked around, sensing the apprehension in O'Flaherty's voice.

"We don't know this sea," Fineen called out.

"Rocks?" Rhattican asked.

"That too, and anything the O'Malleys might scatter to make life difficult to a wayfaring stranger." Fineen was looking anxiously over the side.

"You are close, young man, but you are not there yet," Rhattican said quietly.

"No, he's not," Fineen pointed ahead.

Further in, a boat slowly edged its way out from one of the islands. It seemed to stand-to for a moment, then there was puff of smoke and a dull boom. The cannonball struck the water, leaving them unscathed.

"Fineen!" Rhattican was startled.

"A warning," O'Flaherty assured him. "They're taking their distance. One more shot and they'll have us."

"But," Rhattican began.

"They'll fire or come at us. Either way, we're in trouble," Fineen said grimly.

He looked at Turlough, gave a wry smile, and shook his head.

XXVI

TURLOUGH TOOK hold of Bran Óg and watched as the boat came forward. Now it was clear that there were two master sailors in the Bay, one armed and in home waters, the other unarmed but in a faster boat. All caution was thrown to the wind as Fineen O'Flaherty tacked and railed to escape the other craft.

O'Flaherty's tactics saved his boat. Weaving and ducking between the islands, he gave the O'Malley boat no chance of another clear shot. In this deadly game of hide and seek O'Flaherty seemed in his element; he sat at the helm barking orders to his crew, showing no fear of danger.

"Is he not the fine sailor?" Rhattican declared triumphantly.

"We're both good sailors," Fineen shouted as the Mayo boat came on them again from the port side. "Let us hope no more of them come out. We can dodge one, but if he has aid ..."

Rhattican suddenly stood up in the bow and shouted to Turlough to join him. "Stand here," he said, "and whistle up your dog!"

Bran Óg skidded across the deck and Turlough took him in his arms.

"Now, be still, young fellow, and let them see you," Rhattican directed.

"Why?"

"These Mayo men may be pirates but they do not shoot old men and boys. Not to mention dogs!"

O'Flaherty roared approval from the stern. "You're a crafty one," he shouted.

Turlough looked to their pursuer. There a man was rising to his feet also.

A truce had been called.

Warily the two craft approached each other. When they were within hailing distance the Mayo men accosted them: "What brings you to our waters?"

"O'Flaherty of the Claddagh," Fineen O'Flaherty made himself known.

"An O'Flaherty," the Mayo man said with an expression of distaste. He repeated the name to his crew, then turned back to the Galway boat: "What do you want here?"

"We are unarmed," Fineen pointed out to him.

The Mayo man shook his head. "Heave to," he ordered.

Slowly the helmsmen brought the two boats abreast. The Mayo boat had six on board; lithe, hardy young men, with skins dark from exposure to the Atlantic sea. They looked with open interest at the Galway hooker, clearly intrigued by an O'Flaherty boat carrying an old man, a boy and his dog, a master and two crewmen – and none in a belligerent mood.

For a minute not a word was spoken as the crews eyed each other warily. Rhattican spoke first. "We have come to find the O'Malleys," he said.

"You cannot miss an O'Malley in this place," the Mayo man said slowly.

"I speak to an O'Malley?"

"Why do you ask?"

"We have one of your own with us," Rhattican said, pointing to Turlough.

The O'Malley glanced at Turlough. "This one? He is no O'Malley that I know."

"You don't know me," Turlough said.

This time the O'Malley looked at him more closely. He gave a short smile. "I know I do not. Why so? Where do you hail from?"

"The banks of the Shannon," Rhattican replied.

"Let the boy speak."

Rhattican bowed his head to acknowledge his rudeness.

"Coonagh," Turlough said.

"Where is that?"

"Outside Limerick." Turlough reached beneath his shirt and untied the leather thongs around his waist. He pulled at the thongs until the small leather wallet appeared. Opening the wallet, he took out the medallion given to him by his mother. The O. M. engraving glinted in the sun. He held it out.

The man jerked in surprise, leaned forward and took it from him. He ran his thumb over the surface and said something under his breath.

"Follow us," he said to O'Flaherty and signalled his helmsman to move.

The boats separated and headed for a narrow passage between two islands. The Mayo boat led the way, bringing them in to a small sheltered cove where several boats were tied up. They scrambled across their decks to the shore.

The O'Malleys stood waiting for them. O'Flaherty and the bard were called forward and engaged in conversation with the O'Malley crew. Turlough watched them anxiously; he could only hear indistinct whispers, but he knew from the sharp glances thrown in his direction that he was the subject of their talk. Rhattican looked over at him, a strange expression on his face; there was not a word spoken to him by the others.

A wave of fear swept through Turlough.

The one with the medallion broke away and came forward. Turlough tried to move back but he was not in time. The O'Malley caught him, and swung him up into the air as if he were a small child. Turlough cried out in surprise.

"Thanks be to God!" the O'Malley set Turlough back on the ground.

"I am your uncle, Seamus O'Malley. That ugly bunch," he laughed gaily at the other men, "they are your kinsmen."

He caught Turlough by the shoulder and marched him forward. Bran Óg scampered at their feet, then he broke away and disappeared in a sudden flurry. Turlough walked beside this tall man, his uncle, his eyes taking in these new surroundings. He felt torn between laughter and tears, dizzy with excitement and exhaustion, his journey at an end here in this strange new land.

They left the sea and turned into a boreen, at the end of which stood six small cottages. "Our homes," Seamus said.

As they approached figures appeared from the doorways. From the farthest cottage a tall white-haired woman emerged. Turlough stood stock still. The woman stooped down to pat Bran Óg, who barked happily around her. Turlough's heart stopped. It was his mother?

"Your grandmother," Seamus said quietly and led him forward.

His grandmother held his arms and studied him for a moment. Her eyes were filled with tears. She turned her gaze from Turlough to the door of the cottage.

"And how is the mighty hunter?" came a voice from inside the cabin door.

Turlough could not believe his eyes as the tall figure, Bran Óg sniffing at his shoes, came out from the cabin, holding wide his arms. Turlough ran towards them with a yell of joy.

They hugged each other and all the fear and loneliness seemed to drain away from Turlough as he felt his father's strong arms around him. He heard the laughter of his new-found kinsfolk behind him as they wondered at the events which had brought father and son, each by his own route, to the one place where they could be reunited, a place that each could now call home.

"How?" Turlough began.

"Shhh," his father soothed him. "Yours is the greater story, sure. Mine can wait."

Long hours of talk followed and sometimes Turlough did not know which way to turn, so many eager new faces surrounded him. He told his own story beside a roaring fire with his father by his side and ringed by his O'Malley relations, the proud successors of the famous Granuaile. Then he wanted to hear all about how his father had come to be saved and to arrive safe and sound at the Bay of Islands. But he was also excited to meet his new cousins and they were all showering him with questions.

It was late that night before he finally heard the story of how his father, stunned by a blow to the head, had been left for dead in Limerick. He had regained consciousness that night and had crawled through the confusion and wreckage of the city. But he had failed to make good his escape: caught by soldiers, he had been held prisoner for several months, and forced to work at rebuilding the city's defences for the Ironsides. Only then had he and other prisoners-of-war been released. His journey to the Bay of Islands had been as eventful as Turlough's. He, too, had dodged robbers, renegades and soldiers on his way to the only place he might be safe himself and where, more importantly still, he might meet up, hopefully, with his son.

Just before dawn there was an end of storytelling. A bed had been prepared for Turlough and soon he was able to sleep in comfort at last. But before he slept, tired though he was, he brought to mind his precious memories of his mother, of his Uncle Seán, and of all who had helped him on his way. Now he would hold tightly to himself the memory of them in the peace of his journey's end. And tomorrow he would start a new life in the Bay of Islands.